Certification Study Companion Series

The Apress Certification Study Companion Series offers guidance and hands-on practice to support technical and business professionals who are studying for an exam in the pursuit of an industry certification. Professionals worldwide seek to achieve certifications in order to advance in a career role, reinforce knowledge in a specific discipline, or to apply for or change jobs. This series focuses on the most widely taken certification exams in a given field. It is designed to be user friendly, tracking to topics as they appear in a given exam and work alongside other certification material as professionals prepare for their exam.

More information about this series at https://link.springer.com/bookseries/17100.

Salesforce Developer I Certification

Learn the Basics of Apex, Lightning Web Components, and Flow

Konstantin Kapitanov

Apress®

Salesforce Developer I Certification: Learn the Basics of Apex, Lightning Web Components, and Flow

Konstantin Kapitanov
Borås, Sweden

ISBN-13 (pbk): 979-8-8688-0299-7   ISBN-13 (electronic): 979-8-8688-0300-0
https://doi.org/10.1007/979-8-8688-0300-0

Managing Director, Apress Media LLC: Welmoed Spahr
Acquisitions Editor: Susan McDermott
Development Editor: James Markham
Project Manager: Jessica Vakili

Cover designed by eStudioCalamar

Distributed to the book trade worldwide by Springer Science+Business Media New York, 1 New York Plaza, New York, NY 10004. Phone 1-800-SPRINGER, fax (201) 348-4505, e-mail orders-ny@springer-sbm.com, or visit www.springeronline.com. Apress Media, LLC is a California LLC and the sole member (owner) is Springer Science + Business Media Finance Inc (SSBM Finance Inc). SSBM Finance Inc is a **Delaware** corporation.

For information on translations, please e-mail booktranslations@springernature.com; for reprint, paperback, or audio rights, please e-mail bookpermissions@springernature.com.

Apress titles may be purchased in bulk for academic, corporate, or promotional use. eBook versions and licenses are also available for most titles. For more information, reference our Print and eBook Bulk Sales web page at http://www.apress.com/bulk-sales.

Any source code or other supplementary material referenced by the author in this book is available to readers on the Github repository: https://github.com/Apress/Salesforce-Developer-I-Certification. For more detailed information, please visit https://www.apress.com/gp/services/source-code.

If disposing of this product, please recycle the paper

Table of Contents

About the Author

Konstantin Kapitanov is a certified Salesforce professional based in Sweden with experience and a proven track record of delivering impactful Salesforce solutions and a commitment to innovation. Starting as a web developer, he later founded his consultancy firm, working on CRM projects across Austria, Germany, and Sweden ranging from startups to large enterprises. With a passion for Salesforce, he has successfully developed and implemented tailored solutions over a decade to meet unique business needs. This hands-on experience provided him with a comprehensive understanding of Salesforce from various stakeholders' perspectives. Additionally, he has contributed to IT R&D projects, including open source tools and Progressive Web Application technology for educational materials.

About the Technical Reviewer

 **Ashwini Goudar Siddappa** is a Salesforce expert with experience in the automotive and pharmaceutical industries, demonstrating proficiency in configuration, administration, and development within Salesforce. She possesses a strong grasp of Agile methodologies and is adept in CRM systems, data analysis, process enhancement, and project management. As a certified Salesforce professional, she has demonstrated mastery in various aspects of the platform, making her a trusted authority in the field. Currently, she is working as a Salesforce Chapter Lead in Gothenburg, Sweden.

Preface

Welcome to the world of Salesforce development—a realm of endless possibilities, innovation, and growth. And let me tell you, you're on the right path.

Unlike many resources on the market that dive straight into advanced technical topics, we recognize that every journey begins with a single step. The mission is simple: to provide a welcoming and accessible entry point for non-coder Salesforce professionals, empowering you to take that crucial first step toward Salesforce Developer I certification.

Let's address the elephant in the room—coding. For many non-coders, the thought of diving into the world of programming may seem daunting. Traditional approaches often assume a certain level of technical proficiency, leaving beginners feeling lost in a sea of complex concepts and syntax.

It's understandable that the transition from a non-technical background to a developer role can feel like crossing a vast chasm. That's why this book is crafted as a sturdy bridge—a bridge built upon clarity, encouragement, and a deep understanding of the unique challenges you face.

But why become a Salesforce Developer? What sets this career path apart, and why is Salesforce Developer I certification such an excellent choice for aspiring professionals?

Because it's more than just a job—it's a journey toward empowerment, fulfillment, and endless possibilities.

In today's digital landscape, where businesses strive to stay competitive, Salesforce is revolutionizing how companies engage with their customers, manage their operations, and drive growth. As a Salesforce Developer, you hold the keys to unlocking this transformative potential, shaping the future of businesses across industries.

But beyond the technical skills lies an even greater reward. As a Salesforce Developer, you're not just mastering a set of tools, you're gaining access to a thriving ecosystem of innovation and career growth. With demand for Salesforce expertise soaring, certified developers are in high demand, commanding competitive salaries and endless opportunities for advancement.

Throughout these pages, you'll find a carefully curated roadmap designed to demystify the fundamentals of Salesforce development, from understanding the core concepts of the Salesforce platform to mastering the essentials of Apex and Lightning Web Components guiding you every step of the way.

Welcome to the world of Salesforce development. Your journey starts now.

CHAPTER 1

Salesforce Fundamentals and Architecture

1.1 The Basic Architecture as Model-View-Controller (MVC)

Salesforce is a cloud-based platform that provides customer relationship management (CRM) services to businesses of all sizes. Its architecture is based on the Model-View-Controller (MVC), which separates the data, business logic, and presentation layers of the cloud application. The platform is known for its flexibility, scalability, and customization options. Let's break down the basic architecture of Salesforce, including MVC, multi-tenant environment, and capabilities.

The Model layer refers to the data model consisting of objects, fields, and relationships. Objects represent different types of data, for example, leads, contacts, and accounts. Fields define the attributes of those objects, and relationships establish how different objects are connected to each other, for example, by lookup or master-detail relationships. The Salesforce platform as a component-based framework uses a Salesforce cloud database behind, which is optimized for storing and retrieving data quickly and efficiently. The Salesforce platform allows developers to create custom objects and fields to store data specific to their business needs.

Let's say you're building a custom CRM application in Salesforce. You might create a custom object called "Project__c" to store information about your clients. You can define various fields within this object, such as "Project Name," "Address", "Project Number," and "Project Source." This object definition is part of the Model layer, as it defines the structure of the data you'll be working with.

© Konstantin Kapitanov 2024
K. Kapitanov, *Salesforce Developer I Certification*, Certification Study Companion Series,
https://doi.org/10.1007/979-8-8688-0300-0_1

The View layer in Salesforce refers to the user interface (UI) layer, where users interact with the data in Salesforce platform where reusable UI elements can be combined to create complex interfaces. Lightning Web Components is an advancement of the Lightning Component framework, utilizing modern web standards such as CSS, JavaScript, and HTML. It makes better performance, reusability, and compatibility with other web technologies. The Lightning Design System (SLDS) provides a set of CSS frameworks and design guidelines to ensure consistent branding and user experience across all browsers and mobile applications.

Salesforce generally provides a customizable user interface that allows you to create custom page layouts. These layouts determine which fields are shown, their order, and their formatting. By customizing page layouts, you can tailor the way data is presented to different user profiles and record types. This flexibility allows for a more personalized and efficient user experience within the browser interface.

Salesforce Mobile App provides a mobile-friendly interface for accessing Salesforce on smartphones and tablets. The mobile app interface includes features like responsive layouts, touch gestures, and offline access. It is optimized for smaller screens and touch interactions, providing a seamless and intuitive experience for users on mobile devices.

The Controller layer in Salesforce refers to the business logic layer, where application logic responsible for handling user interactions, processing data, and coordinating the flow of information between the model and the view is implemented. Salesforce provides a set of declarative tools to create logic and automation without the need for coding. Developers can also use Apex, a Java-like programming language, to create custom code to implement more complex business logic.

By executing logic, for instance, you have a requirement to automatically convert a Lead into an Opportunity when certain conditions are met. The Controller layer would handle the logic to create the Opportunity record and associate it with the relevant data from the Lead. Controllers can also be used to integrate Salesforce with external systems. If your application needs to communicate with an external REST API, you might implement the logic to make HTTP Callouts, receive and process the response, and update Salesforce records based on the external data.

Model-View-Controller		
Model Layer	*Controller Layer*	**View Layer**
Objects	*Classes*	Visualforce pages
Fields	*Triggers*	Lightning Components
Relationships	*Methods*	Mobile Apps

Figure 1-1. *Model-View-Controller architecture*

1.2 Multi-tenant Environment and Its Implications

Salesforce operates in a multi-tenant environment, which refers to a software architecture where a single instance of a software application serves multiple customers or tenants organizations simultaneously. Imagine a bank that offers safe-deposit boxes to its customers. Each customer can rent a safe-deposit box to store their valuable items, documents, and assets. The bank provides a secure and controlled environment where each box is protected with individual keys and locks. Customers have exclusive access to their own box, and the bank ensures the privacy and security of their belongings.
In a multi-tenant environment, a single instance of a software application or platform is shared by multiple users or tenants. Each tenant is a separate entity with its own data, configurations, and customizations. Just like the safe-deposit boxes in the bank, each tenant's data is isolated from other tenants. The software platform ensures that tenants cannot access or interfere with each other's data. The integrity of each tenant's data is protected from Salesforce. Multi-tenancy is an integral part of the Salesforce architecture, and this allows to provide economies of scale and reduce costs for customers. To operate as a multi-tenant platform has several implications, especially

- *Shared Resources*: In a multi-tenant environment, hardware, databases, and infrastructure are shared among multiple organizations. This pooling of resources can lead to cost savings and efficient resource utilization.

3

- *Data Isolation*: Each tenant's data is logically separated and isolated from other tenants' data. This isolation is crucial to maintain data privacy and security. But all tenants share a multitenant database that can store tenant-specific data, metadata, and customizations.

- *Scalability*: Multi-tenant environments can scale horizontally, allowing new tenants to be added without requiring significant changes to the underlying infrastructure. This is especially beneficial for cloud-based platforms that need to accommodate a growing customer database.

- *Customization and Configuration*: Despite sharing the same application instance, each tenant can customize and configure the platform to meet their specific needs. Salesforce provides tools like custom objects, fields, Flows, and Apex code to enable this customization.

- *Upgrade and Maintenance*: Upgrades and maintenance tasks can be performed centrally by Salesforce. This ensures that all tenants have access to the latest features, bug fixes, and security patches without requiring individual updates for each organization.

- *Data Security and Compliance*: Salesforce employs rigorous security measures to ensure that each tenant's data remains secure and compliant with industry standards and regulations. Data encryption, access controls, and auditing are integral to maintaining security.

Figure 1-2. *Multi-tenant environment*

1.3 Salesforce Clouds and Extensions

Salesforce offers a variety of clouds and extensions that provide different capabilities for businesses. The major clouds include but are not limited to Sales Cloud, Service Cloud, Experience Cloud, Marketing Cloud, Commerce Cloud, and CRM Analytics. There are also some additional clouds designed to empower different types of businesses and organizations. For more actual insight check directly www.salesforce.com/products/.

Salesforce AppExchange is an enterprise cloud marketplace that offers ready-to-install apps and solutions to extend Salesforce into every aspect of the business. It is the largest and most well-established cloud marketplace created. For more details see https://appexchange.salesforce.com/.

In this book, we will be using Salesforce Developer Edition as the primary platform for exercising and practicing various Salesforce development concepts. It is important to set up this edition before starting the exercises to ensure that you can follow along with the examples and exercises laid out in the book.

Salesforce Developer Edition is a free, fully functional version of the Salesforce platform that developers can use to build and test applications. It is often used by individual developers or small teams to build and test applications before deploying them to production. Developer Edition orgs are isolated from other orgs and can be used for learning, prototyping, and developing proof-of-concepts. It provides access to all the features and functionality of Salesforce, including the ability to create custom objects, Flows, and triggers. By using Salesforce Developer Edition, you will have a safe and secure environment to practice building and testing your Salesforce applications. It will also allow you to experiment with different features and functionalities without affecting your production environment.

To set up Salesforce Developer Edition, you will need to create a free account on Salesforce's website `https://developer.salesforce.com/signup`. Once you have set up your account, you will have access to your own personal Salesforce org, where you can begin practicing and building your Salesforce applications.

CHAPTER 2

Objects and Data Management

2.1 Standard and Customer Objects

Salesforce objects and fields are analogous to database tables and the table columns. Objects are tables that store specific data in Salesforce. The Salesforce platform has standard objects and custom objects. Standard objects are objects that are included with Salesforce, while custom objects are objects that are created by users to store information unique to their organization. Object fields are the individual data points that make up an object, and object relationships define how objects are related to each other. Important standard objects in Salesforce include but not limited to:

> *Account*: This object stores information about customers, partners, competitors, or other organizations.

> *Contact*: This object represents individuals associated with an account.

> *Opportunity:* This object tracks potential sales deals and includes information such as deal value, stage, and close date.

> *Lead*: This object stores information about potential customers or prospects.

> *Product*: This object represents the products or services offered by a company.

> *Campaign*: This object tracks marketing campaigns and their associated leads and opportunities.

© Konstantin Kapitanov 2024
K. Kapitanov, *Salesforce Developer I Certification*, Certification Study Companion Series, https://doi.org/10.1007/979-8-8688-0300-0_2

Case: This object is used for tracking and managing customer support issues or inquiries.

User: This object represents individual users of the Salesforce platform.

Contract: This object stores information about contracts or agreements with customers.

Report and Dashboard: These objects allow users to create and view data analytics.

These standard objects provide a foundation for managing various aspects of a business within the Salesforce platform. The difference between standard and custom objects in Salesforce can be summarized as follows:

Standard objects are pre-built objects that come included with Salesforce. These objects have a set of default fields and functionality that can be used out-of-the-box. Standard objects are designed to handle common business processes and are already configured in the Salesforce platform.

Custom objects are objects that users can create themselves to store information specific to their organization. Users can define their own fields, relationships, and logic within custom objects. Custom objects allow for the customization and extension of the Salesforce platform to meet specific business needs. They provide a structure for sharing data and can be tailored to fit unique requirements. Custom objects are the heart of any application built on the Salesforce platform.

To create a custom object, go to Setup ➤ Object Manager tab, and click the "Create" button.

In Salesforce, both standard and custom objects have APIs (Application Programming Interfaces) that allow developers to interact with and manipulate the data and functionality of these objects programmatically. The API names for standard objects are well-defined and consistent, while custom object API names are based on the name provided when the custom object is created. Here are some examples of standard object API names in Salesforce:

Account: API Name: Account

Contact: API Name: Contact

Opportunity: API Name: Opportunity

For custom objects, the API name typically ends with __c to denote that it's a custom object. For example, if you create a custom object called "Project," its API name might be Project__c.

It's important to note that these API names are used developing custom code such as Apex triggers or Lightning Web Components (LWC), integrating with external systems, and performing data manipulation. These API names provide a standardized way to reference and interact with objects and their data in the Salesforce platform.

2.2 Fields and Relationships

Fields are columns on an object, which can be used for individual data records stored in an object. They define the specific attributes or characteristics of the data you want to capture. Each field has a data type that determines the kind of data it can store like text, number, date, picklist, and other.

Standard fields are those that are already present in the Salesforce when a new organization is created. They are present in all organizations where the same features are enabled. These fields cannot be customized to the same degree as custom fields. For example, you can change the display label, but not the underlying API name or data type.

Custom fields are fields that have been added to the standard Salesforce schema to tailor the data for each object. The user who creates the field can specify the field type and any applicable limitations such as the maximum number of characters in a text field. Overall, custom fields provide more flexibility and customization options than standard fields, but both are integral to managing data in Salesforce. You can query standard and custom fields and objects using SOQL in the same way. We will come to this in the next chapter.

Relationships define how different objects are related to each other. In Salesforce, you can establish relationships between objects to represent connections between data records.

Master relationship is a type of object relationship that is used to define the relationship between a master or parent and a detail or child object. The master object controls certain behaviors of the detail object such as if record of the master object is deleted, its related detail records are also deleted, or managing sharing and security settings. Additionally, the owner field on the detail object is not available and is automatically set to the owner of its associated master record. Master-detail relationships can exist between a standard object as master and a custom object as detail, or between two custom objects. Each detail record must be associated with a master record, establishing a hierarchical relationship. Importantly, standard objects cannot be on the detail side of a relationship with a custom object. When a master record is deleted, its detail records are automatically deleted due to the master-detail relationship. In all cases of master-detail relationships, the connection is established through a relationship field on the detail object. These relationships enforce data integrity and enable special features like roll-up summaries and cascading deletions.

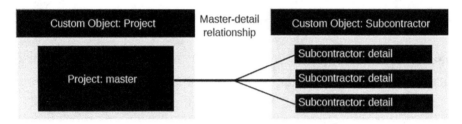

Figure 2-1. *Master relationship between two objects*

Lookup relationships are a way to link two objects together. They are similar to master-detail relationships, but they do not support sharing and security settings or roll-up summary fields. A lookup relationship is a loosely connected relationship that enables one-to-many connections between objects. It allows you to connect one object to another in a one-to-many fashion. In a lookup relationship, one object has a field that references the field of another object. This field is called a lookup field, and it allows you to look up records on another object. For example, account as standard object represents company records, and project as custom object represents individual projects associated with specific accounts. Each account can have multiple associated project records, as indicated by the lookup relationship in the project object. Deleting an account does not automatically delete associated project records, as lookup relationships do not enforce cascading deletion. Projects remain intact even if the associated account is deleted.

Many-to-many relationships in Salesforce allow each record of one object to be linked to multiple records from another object and vice versa. To create a many-to-many relationship in Salesforce, a junction object is needed. A junction object is a custom object that links two other objects together. This means that multiple records from one object can be associated with multiple records from another object. For example, let's say we have two objects: "Books" and "Authors." A book can have multiple authors, and an author can have written multiple books. In this scenario, we would create a junction object called "Book Author" to establish a many-to-many relationship between the "Books" and "Authors" objects.

Many-to-many relationships are useful when dealing with complex data structures and can help to simplify data management.

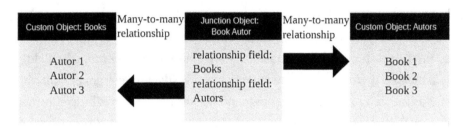

Figure 2-2. *Many-to-many relationship with junction object*

A hierarchical relationship is a special type of relationship that is related only to the user object in Salesforce. It allows users to use a lookup field to associate one user with another that does not directly or indirectly refer to itself. For example, you can create a custom hierarchical relationship field to store each user's direct manager.

It is a type of advanced relationship that is on top of the parent-child relationship, which includes the master-detail and lookup relationships.

Salesforce allows users to create customized fields that can be used to calculate and summarize data. Two types of such fields are the formula field and the roll-up summary field.

A formula field is a read-only field that derives its value from a formula expression that you define. A formula can reference fields from the same object, related parent object, and other objects. They can be created on standard or custom objects, and fields can be of different data types. Some common use cases for formula fields include but are not limited to

- *Calculating of Total Price*: You can create a formula field that multiplies the quantity and unit price fields to calculate the total price of a product in an Opportunity or Quote record.

- *Time Duration Calculation*: A formula field can determine the contact duration based on their completion and the current date.

- *Concatenating Text*: You can create a formula field to combine text from multiple fields, such as creating a full name field by combining first name and last name fields.

- *Conditional Logic*: Formulas can include IF statements and logical operators to display different values based on certain conditions.

A roll-up summary field is used to calculate the COUNT, SUM, MIN, or MAX of fields values in the child records of a master-detail relationship. Roll-up summary fields can only be created on the master object of a master-detail relationship to summarize fields on the child object that are themselves not formula fields or fields that reference other objects. Formula fields that reference other objects can't be summarized in roll-up summary fields.

Both these field types are useful in simplifying data entry and automating calculations in Salesforce.

To create formula or roll-up summary fields, access the Object Manager from Setup and navigate to the object you wish to create the formula field on. Then, select Fields and Relationships on the left menu, and click the button New.

2.3 Data Management Tools

The *Schema Builder* is a visual tool within Salesforce that provides a graphical representation of your organization's data model. It allows you to create, modify, and view objects, fields, and relationships in a visual interface. With the Schema Builder, you can

Add Objects: Create new custom objects with fields and relationships.

Add Fields: Define the fields for each object, specifying data types and properties.

Create Relationships: Establish relationships between objects using lookup or master-detail relationships.

View Object Dependencies: See how objects are related to each other in a visual diagram.

Plan Data Model: Plan and design your organization's data structure before implementing changes.

> *Entity Relationship Diagram (ERD) Creation*: Schema builder can
> be used to create an ERD that illustrates a particular feature for
> the client.

The Schema Builder is a powerful tool for administrators and developers to design and manage the data architecture of their Salesforce organization in a user-friendly and intuitive manner. It helps ensure that your data is organized, structured, and related correctly, which is crucial for effective data management and application development.

You can go to Setup ➤ Type "Schema Builder" in quick find box on the left.

The *Data Import Wizard* is a tool within Salesforce that allows users to import data from a CSV (comma-separated values) file into their Salesforce organization. It is an efficient and user-friendly tool that can be accessed directly from Salesforce Setup, without any additional configuration needed. The tool provides a unified interface through which users can import data for accounts and contacts, leads, solutions, and custom objects. With the Data Import Wizard, users can seamlessly import, update, or upsert data into multiple standard objects and custom objects within their Salesforce org, up to 50,000 records per import. The tool also enables users to compare their data fields with the Salesforce fields they can import into and verify that their data will be mapped into the appropriate Salesforce fields. Users can make any necessary configuration changes in Salesforce to handle the imported data.

You can go to Setup ➤ Type "Data Import Wizard" in quick find box on the left.

A *Data Loader* is a software tool that enables automated, high-volume import, export, and storage of Salesforce data. It is used for bulk importing and exporting of data. Data Loader reads, extracts, and loads data from comma-separated values (CSV) files during the import process, or from a database connection. It allows users to add, update, and edit large amounts of data at once and supports operations such as inserting, updating, deleting, and exporting data. Users can map fields, transform data, and automate operations using the command line interface. It is important to note that Data Loader is different from the Data Import Wizard. The Data Import Wizard makes it easy to import data for many standard Salesforce objects, including accounts, contacts, leads, campaign members, and another. You can also import data for custom objects and can import up to 50,000 records at a time. In contrast, Data Loader allows users to load up to 150 million records and supports more complex imports of data.

Data Export refers to the process of exporting and creating backups of your organization's data from your Salesforce instance to an external location. It allows you to capture a snapshot of your data at a specific point in time, which is crucial for data backup, recovery, compliance, and data migration purposes. Salesforce offers a built-in Data Export feature that enables you to export your data in a structured format, typically in CSV file. Users can export data manually or schedule automatic exports like weekly or monthly intervals. It's important to note that while Data Export is useful for creating backups and snapshots, it might not be the ideal solution for all data integration or synchronization needs. For more complex data operations, you might consider using other tools such as Salesforce Data Loader, third-party integration platforms, or custom development using Salesforce APIs.

You can go to Setup ➤ Type "Data Export" in the search field on the left menu.

Mass Delete Records refers to the process of deleting a large number of records from one or more objects in a single operation. This feature is particularly useful when you need to remove multiple records that meet certain criteria or are no longer needed, saving time and effort compared to manually deleting records one by one. It's important to exercise caution when using the Mass Delete Records feature, as deleted data cannot always be fully recovered. Always carefully review the criteria and records that will be affected before confirming a mass delete operation. Additionally, it's a good practice to perform a backup or export of the data you intend to delete before proceeding. Mass Delete Records is a powerful tool for data management in Salesforce, but it should be used thoughtfully and responsibly to ensure data accuracy and integrity.

You can go to Setup ➤ Type "Mass Delete Records" in the search field on the left menu.

Workbench is a free web-based tool that offers a variety of functionalities for interacting with your Salesforce organization's data, metadata, and APIs.

It can be used for data management activities such as bulk record updates, mass creation, and mass deletion by bringing together a variety of really useful capabilities in a single tool. It allows users to perform data manipulation language (DML) operations and can retrieve and deploy the metadata of custom applications, objects, and other components using Metadata API. Workbench is a powerful tool for Salesforce administrators and developers to manage their data and metadata in a user-friendly and intuitive manner.

workbench ⬡ ▾   info ▾   queries ▾   data ▾   migration ▾   utilities ▾

KONSTANTIN KAPITANOV AT BD ON API 58.0

Environment: Production ▾

API Version: 58.0 ▾

☑ I agree to the terms of service

Workbench is free to use, but is not an official salesforce.com product. Workbench has not been officially tested or documented. salesforce.com support is not available for Workbench. Support requests for Workbench should be directed to Stackoverflow at https://salesforce.stackexchange.com/questions/tagged/workbench. Source code for Workbench can be found at https://github.com/forceworkbench/forceworkbench under separate and different license terms.

Login with Salesforce

Requested in 0.003 sec
Workbench 58.0.0

See more details here https://workbench.developerforce.com.

CHAPTER 3

Salesforce Automatization Tools

3.1 Quick Actions, Page Layouts, and Record Types

Quick Actions, Page Layouts, and Record Types are features that play a crucial role in defining how users interact with records and perform actions within the application. They contribute to creating a tailored user experience by determining what information is displayed and what actions are available on a record's detail page.

Quick Actions in Salesforce are a feature that allows users to perform specific tasks or actions quickly and efficiently within the Salesforce platform and mobile app without navigating away from the current page. These actions can be standard or custom, and they provide a streamlined way for users to perform common tasks. Common examples of Quick Actions include but are not limited to:

Create a Record: Users can quickly create a new related record, like a new Task or Event, directly from the record's detail page.

Log a Call: Users can log call details, including notes, outcome, and duration, with a single click.

Send Email: Users can send an email to a contact or lead without leaving the current page.

Update a Record: Users can change the status of a record, like marking a Lead as qualified.

A "Create Feed Item" is an option on a Quick Action in Salesforce which allows users to create a post on the Chatter feed related to a record or object. This can be useful for sharing information or updates with other users who are following the record or object.

© Konstantin Kapitanov 2024
K. Kapitanov, *Salesforce Developer I Certification*, Certification Study Companion Series,
https://doi.org/10.1007/979-8-8688-0300-0_3

This option is available when creating a Quick Action on an object, and can be selected as an option when configuring the action.

Page Layouts define the organization and arrangement of fields, sections, related lists, and quick actions on a record's detail page. They determine what information is displayed to users and how it's presented. Page layouts can be customized to match the needs of different user profiles, record types, and applications. Key components of a Page Layout include but are not limited to

> *Fields*: The individual data fields like Name, Phone, and Email displayed on the page

> *Sections*: Groups of related fields organized together for better readability

> *Related Lists*: Lists of related records, such as open activities, closed activities, and related records

For instance, you might create different page layouts for different types of Opportunities, ensuring that each layout shows the most relevant fields and actions for that Opportunity type. You can also tailor page layouts based on user profiles, presenting only the information and actions that are relevant to a specific role or department.

Record Types allow you to define different sets of picklist values, page layouts, and business processes for different types of records within the same object. For example, in an Opportunity object, you might have different record types for "New Business" and "Renewal" opportunities, each with its own set of fields and page layouts. Users can select the appropriate record type when creating a new record, ensuring that it aligns with the specific requirements of their task or scenario.

Quick Actions, Page Layouts, and Record Types contribute to improving user efficiency and user adoption by providing a customized and efficient interface for interacting with records. They help users focus on the tasks they need to complete while avoiding unnecessary clutter and complexity.

To create Quick Actions, Page Layouts, and Record Types, select first the object you want to create on. Then, in Object Manager on the left menu, click Page Layouts or Buttons, Links, and Actions to create Quick Actions or create new Record Types, and specify the picklist values, page layouts, and other settings unique to each record type.

3.2 Validation Roles and Approval Processes

Validation rules in Salesforce are business rules that ensure the accuracy and integrity of data before it is saved. They act as checkpoints to verify whether the data being entered meets the standards set by the organization. Validation rules can contain formulas or expressions that evaluate the data in one or more fields and return a value of "True" or "False." If the data does not meet the specified criteria, a user-friendly error message is displayed, prompting the user to correct it. Validation rules can be applied at the object level, and they can be used to enforce integrity constraints against the data. Additionally, validation rules can be used to make fields required for certain users based on their roles.

Example of a Validation Rule:

Suppose you have a custom object called "Candidate__c" with a field "Years_of_Experience__c." You want to prevent users from saving a candidate record if the years of experience are negative. You can create a validation rule with the following formula: Years_of_Experience__c < 0.

To create validation rules, select first the object you want to create. Then in Object Manager on the left menu, click Validation Rules.

Approval Processes automate the process of submitting, reviewing, and approving records. Records submitted for approval are approved by users in the organization, called approvers. They are commonly used for scenarios like deal approvals, expense report approvals, or any process that requires multiple levels of approval. Key points about Approval Processes:

> *Approval Steps*: Approval Processes consist of one or more approval steps. Each step can have multiple approvers and conditions that determine when it's triggered.

> *Submit for Approval*: Users initiate the approval process by submitting a record for approval. The process then follows the defined approval steps.

> *Email Notifications*: Approvers receive email notifications when they have pending approval requests. They can approve, reject, or request changes to the record.

Automated Actions: You can define automated actions that occur after approval or rejection, such as field updates or sending follow-up emails.

Final Approval or Rejection: Once a record reaches the final approval step and is approved, it's marked as "Approved." If rejected, it's marked as "Rejected."

Example of an Approval Process

Imagine you have a custom object "Expense_Report__c" that tracks employee expense submissions. You want to automate the approval process for these reports. You can create an approval process with two steps: "Manager Approval" and "Finance Approval." Each step has specific criteria for when it should trigger and who should approve. Approval Processes streamline and enforce consistent approval workflows while providing transparency into the approval status of records.

To create approval processes, you can go to Setup ➤ Type "Approval Processes" in the search field on the left menu.

Both Validation Rules and Approval Processes contribute to the customization and automation of Salesforce, allowing organizations to align the platform with their specific business processes and ensure data accuracy and compliance.

3.3 Declarative Programming with Flows

With retirement of Process Builder and Workflow Rules, the creation of new processes is limited. So now, new processes can only be created using Flow.

The Migrate to Flow is an official tool provided by Salesforce to assist with the migration of workflow rules to flows. It is designed to help users transition their existing workflow rules and processes to the newer flow automation tool in Salesforce.

Go to Setup ➤ Type "Migrate to Flow" in the search field on the left menu.

Flows is a tool within the Salesforce platform that allows to automate complex business processes. It collects data and performs actions based on that data. Flow Builder is the declarative interface used to create individual flows, enabling users to build code-like logic without using a programming language. Some of the key benefits include

Automating Business Processes: Salesforce Flow allows users to automate complex business processes by collecting data and performing actions based on that data. It provides a visual interface for defining the sequence of steps and conditions, making it easier to create custom workflows that guide users through tasks efficiently and consistently.

Collecting and Updating Data: Flow enables to collect and manipulate data without the need for coding. It provides variables to store and manipulate data throughout the flow, and actions to perform specific activities such as creating records or updating fields. This allows to streamline data collection and update processes within the Salesforce platform.

Integration with Other Salesforce Features: Salesforce Flow can be seamlessly integrated with other Salesforce tools and features. This integration capability allows to leverage the full power of the Salesforce platform and create comprehensive process automations.

User Interactions: Flow provides the ability to create quick screens for user interactions. This allows end users to input data and interact with the flow, making the automation process more user-friendly and intuitive. Users can create screens with input fields, picklists, checkboxes, and other components to gather the necessary information for the process.

Code-Free Automation: One of the major advantages of Salesforce Flow is its declarative nature, which means users can build code-like logic without the need for extensive coding knowledge. This empowers to create powerful process automations without writing complex code, making it accessible to a wider range of users.

Salesforce offers different types of flows that cater to various automation needs. See the available types of Flows on the following diagram. Each type of flow serves a specific purpose and can be used to automate different aspects of business processes within the Salesforce platform.

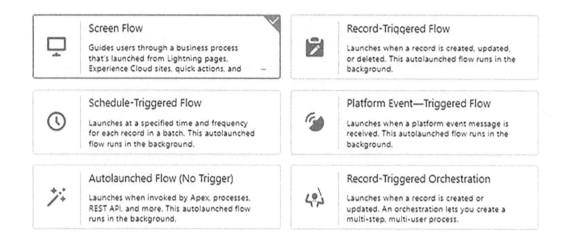

Screen Flows are a type of flow that allows you to create interactive, guided experiences for users. They're designed to gather and display information from users in a step-by-step manner, guiding them through a series of screens to accomplish a specific task or provide information. Screen Flows are particularly useful for creating user-friendly data entry forms, wizards, and self-service processes. Here's how Screen Flows work and their key features:

- *Interactive Steps*: Screen Flows are composed of individual screens that users interact with. Each screen can present information, ask for input, and guide users through a specific action.

- *Visual Design*: Flow Builder provides a drag-and-drop interface for designing the layout and content of each screen. You can arrange fields, buttons, images, and text to create a visually appealing and user-friendly experience.

- *Input Elements*: Screens can include various input elements, such as text fields, picklists, buttons, and checkboxes. Users can provide data directly within the flow.

- *Data Validation*: You can apply validation rules to the input fields to ensure that users provide accurate and complete information. If a user enters invalid data, the flow can display error messages.

- *Conditional Logic*: Screens can use conditional logic to dynamically show or hide components based on user selections or previous inputs. This helps create a personalized experience.

- *Navigation and Flow Control*: You can define the flow's behavior by adding decision elements that determine which screen to display next based on user inputs. This enables you to create branching paths within the flow.

- *Record Creation and Updates*: Screen Flows can create new records or update existing records in Salesforce. Users can enter data, which the flow uses to populate fields in the target record.

- *Integration*: Screen Flows can integrate with external services, APIs, and databases to fetch or send data as part of the flow.

- *Guided Experience*: Screen Flows guide users through a series of sequential steps, reducing the risk of errors and ensuring a consistent process.

- *Mobile and Lightning Experience*: Screen Flows are optimized for mobile devices and Salesforce Lightning Experience, making them suitable for both desktop and mobile users.

Some examples of use cases for Screen Flows include

- *Data Entry and Updates*: Use Screen Flows to create intuitive data entry forms for users to create or update records.

- *Self-service Processes*: Build self-service wizards that guide customers through tasks like submitting support requests or updating their account information.

- *Lead and Case Qualification*: Create guided processes to qualify leads or cases based on specific criteria and user input.

- *Employee Onboarding*: Design onboarding processes that guide new employees through providing information and completing necessary forms.

Record-Triggered Flows are a type of flow that are initiated and executed in response to changes made to records. Unlike autolaunched flows that are programmatically triggered, record-triggered flows are directly associated with specific objects and are triggered when records of those objects are created or updated. They are designed to automate processes and actions that are closely tied to record changes, allowing you to perform complex logic and updates. Here are the key features for Record-Triggered Flows:

- *Record-Driven Execution*: Record-triggered flows are started by the creation or modification of records of a specific object.

- *Real-Time Automation*: These flows can respond to changes in real time, allowing you to implement immediate updates and actions based on record changes.

- *Change-Based Logic*: You can define different logic and actions to occur based on the values of fields before and after the record change.

- *Before-Save and After-Save Logic*: Record-triggered flows can be set to run either before or after the record is saved, giving you control over when the flow's actions occur.

- *Complex Logic*: Implement complex decision-making, branching, and multiple actions within a single flow based on the record's changes.

- *Updates and Notifications*: Use record-triggered flows to update related records, send notifications, create tasks, and perform other actions based on the changes.

- *Integration with Apex*: You can invoke record-triggered flows from Apex triggers, or other flow types to create a comprehensive automation strategy.

Some examples of use cases for Record-Triggered Flows include

- *Field Updates*: Automatically update related fields or records when specific fields change on a record.

- *Validation and Data Cleaning*: Implement complex data validation rules that check multiple fields and conditions before allowing a record to be saved.

- *Approval Workflows*: Implement customized approval processes and notifications based on changes to approval-related fields.

- *Notification and Follow-Up*: Automatically send emails or notifications to users or customers based on changes to records.

- *Cascade Updates*: Update related records when a parent record changes, ensuring data consistency.

Schedule-Triggered Flows allow you to automate processes and perform actions on a scheduled basis. Unlike other types of flows that are triggered by user interactions or record changes, schedule-triggered flows are initiated based on a predefined schedule, such as a specific date and time or a recurring interval. They are especially useful for automating repetitive tasks, time-based actions, and batch processing. Here are the key features for Schedule-Triggered Flows:

- *Scheduled Automation*: Schedule-Triggered Flows are designed to run at specific times or intervals without requiring manual user intervention. You can define when the flow should run, such as daily, weekly, or on a specific date.

- *Time-Based Logic*: These flows can incorporate time-based logic to determine which actions to take based on the current date, time, or day of the week.

- *Batch Processing*: Schedule-Triggered Flows can process records in batches, allowing you to handle a large volume of records in chunks, which is particularly useful for data cleanup, maintenance, and updates.

- *Record Updates and Actions*: Use these flows to update records, send email notifications, create tasks, and perform various other actions on a scheduled basis.

- *Recurrence Patterns*: You can define recurring schedules using patterns like daily, weekly, monthly, or annually. For example, you can schedule a flow to run every Monday at 10:00 AM.

- *Time Zone Considerations*: The flow's scheduled run times are based on the organization's time zone settings, ensuring that the automation aligns with your business hours.

- *Start and End Dates*: Specify a start date and, if needed, an end date to control the period during which the flow should run.

Some examples of use cases for Schedule-Triggered Flows include

- *Data Maintenance*: Automate data cleanup tasks like archiving old records, updating expired records, or removing duplicates.

- *Follow-Up Communications*: Send follow-up emails to customers after specific events or milestones, such as purchase confirmation emails.

- *Reminders*: Create scheduled reminders for users to review or take action on records after a certain period of time.

- *Recurring Tasks*: Automate tasks like data backups, report generation, and record updates on a regular basis.

- *Time-Dependent Workflows*: Use schedule-triggered flows as an alternative to time-dependent workflow rules, providing greater flexibility and capabilities.

Autolaunched Flows are a type of flow that can be initiated and executed without any direct user interaction or record-based trigger. Unlike other flow types that are triggered by user actions or record changes, autolaunched flows are designed to be started and executed programmatically and implementing business logic without user interface elements. Here are the key features for Autolaunched Flows:

- *Programmatic Execution*: Autolaunched flows are intended to be initiated and executed programmatically using various tools and integrations within Salesforce.

- *External System Integration*: These flows can be triggered by external systems or events, allowing you to integrate with third-party applications, services, or custom processes.

- *Automation*: Autolaunched flows are a way to encapsulate and automate complex processes that involve multiple steps, decision-making, and interactions.

- *Data Manipulation*: You can use autolaunched flows to manipulate data, perform calculations, update records, send notifications, and more.

- *Record Creation and Updates*: Autolaunched flows can create new records or update existing records based on predefined logic.

Some examples of use cases for Autolaunched Flows include

- *Integration with External Systems*: Initiate flows based on events or data changes from external systems to keep data synchronized.

- *Data Migration*: Use flows to transform and migrate data from one object or system to another.

- *Data Enrichment*: Automatically enrich records by querying external data sources and updating records with additional information.

- *Complex Logic*: Implement complex business logic that involves decision-making, multiple steps, and interactions without direct user input.

- *Mass Updates*: Use flows to update a large number of records with specific criteria in a controlled and automated manner.

Platform Event-Triggered Flow in Salesforce Flow Builder combines the capabilities of platform events and flows to automate processes based on the occurrence of platform events. A platform event is a custom object in Salesforce used to publish and subscribe to events within the Salesforce ecosystem and between Salesforce and external systems. Platform Event-Triggered Flows allow you to automate actions and logic in response to the publishing of platform events. Here are the key features of Event-Triggered Flows:

- *Platform Event*: A platform event is a structured message representing an occurrence in Salesforce or an external system. Platform events are used to communicate changes or events in a loosely coupled manner.

- *Flow Automation*: Platform Event-Triggered Flows automate actions based on the publication of platform events. When a platform event is published, the flow is triggered to execute its defined actions.

- *Event-Driven Logic*: The flow's logic and actions are executed in response to specific platform event occurrences, enabling you to perform complex and targeted automation.

- *Record Updates and Actions*: Just like other flow types, Platform Event-Triggered Flows can update records, create records, send notifications, and perform various actions based on the event's data.

- *Decoupled Architecture*: Platform events facilitate communication between different systems, applications, or components without tight dependencies.

- *External System Integration*: Platform events can be consumed and published by external systems, allowing for seamless integration between Salesforce and external systems.

Some examples of use cases for Event-Triggered Flows include

- *Real-Time Integration*: Integrate Salesforce with external systems by triggering flows based on events occurring in external systems or vice versa.

- *Cross-Object Updates*: Automate updates to related records based on events that occur in other records.

- *Complex Logic*: Implement business processes that require dynamic and complex decision-making based on event data.

- *Data Synchronization*: Keep data synchronized between different systems by using platform events as a communication mechanism.

- *Custom Notifications*: Trigger custom notifications or alerts based on specific event occurrences.

Record-Triggered Orchestration is an advanced feature that allows you to create a coordinated sequence of flows and actions in response to changes made to records. It enables you to design complex automation scenarios that involve multiple flows, each responsible for specific tasks, and orchestrate their execution based on record changes.

Record-Triggered Orchestration helps you break down complex processes into modular and manageable components, making it easier to maintain, update, and scale your automation efforts. Here's how Record-Triggered Orchestration works:

- *Multiple Flows*: With Record-Triggered Orchestration, you can create multiple flows, each focusing on a specific task or set of actions.

- *Trigger Logic*: You define the logic that determines which flows should be executed based on the changes made to records. Each flow can be triggered by specific criteria.

- *Flow Interaction*: Flows within the orchestration can interact with each other by passing data between them using flow variables.

- *Sequential Execution*: The flows within the orchestration are executed in a specified sequence, allowing you to ensure that tasks are performed in the desired order.

- *Conditional Flow Execution*: You can incorporate decision elements to conditionally execute specific flows based on certain conditions or outcomes from earlier flows.

- *Parallel Execution*: If needed, you can design the orchestration to execute multiple flows in parallel, allowing for more efficient and simultaneous processing.

Some examples of use cases for Record-Triggered Orchestration include

- *Complex Processes*: Orchestration is useful for automating processes that involve multiple steps, data updates, notifications, and integrations.

- *Cross-Object Actions*: Automate actions on multiple related records in response to changes in one record.

- *Consistency and Compliance*: Enforce consistent and compliant processes across your organization by orchestrating multiple flows to handle different aspects of a process.

- *Data Transformation and Enrichment*: Perform data transformations and enrichments across various records within a single orchestrated automation.

3.4 Flow Components

Salesforce Flow consists of several components that work together to automate business processes. These components include elements, variables, and connectors.

Elements represent the actions that the flow can execute. Elements are connected together to define the flow's sequence and logic, determining the order in which actions are executed. There are different types of elements available in Salesforce Flow, depending on the type of flow being created. Some examples of elements include

- *Screen Elements*: These elements are used to display screens to users and collect data from them.

- *Action Elements*: Action elements allow users to perform specific actions, such as sending emails, creating records, or executing custom Apex code.

- *Logic Elements*: Logic elements enable users to define conditions and perform branching or decision-making within the flow.

- *Data Elements*: Data elements are used to manipulate and update data within the flow, such as updating record fields or performing calculations.

Variables and resources store and manipulate data throughout the flow. They can hold values, formulas, formatted text, records, or collections of records. Variables and resources allow users to store and reference data at different stages of the flow, enabling data manipulation and decision-making based on stored values.

Connectors define the path that the flow takes as it runs. They connect elements together and guide the flow's execution from one element to the next. Connectors play a crucial role in controlling the flow's sequence and determining the path it follows based on the defined logic.

By utilizing elements, variables, resources, and connectors, you can create powerful and customized flows to automate complex business processes within the Salesforce platform. These components work together to collect and update data, interact with users, and define the flow's logic and execution path.

3.5 Building a Flow

Now, we want to create a simple flow in Flow Builder that automatically creates a new task on the account from the related opportunity based on when the opportunity reaches a Negotiation/Review stage.

Note! Remember that certain features and permissions may vary based on your Salesforce edition, customization, and the organization's configuration. It is a best practice to develop and test flows in a sandbox environment before deploying them to a production environment. This approach helps ensure the stability and reliability of the flow before it is used in production environment where data integrity and user experience are critical.

Step 1: Choosing a "Record-Triggered Flow" is a suitable choice because Record-Triggered Flows have access to the entire record context, both old and new field values. This allows you to evaluate changes in the opportunity record, such as the stage reaching a certain value. Now click Create button as follows.

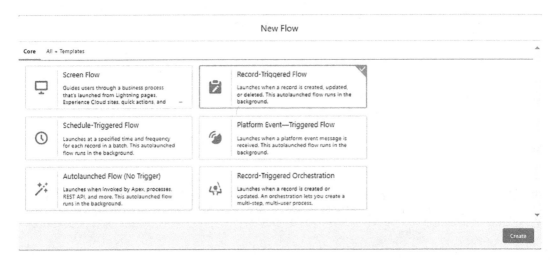

Step 2: In the new dialog window, choose Select Object ➤ "Opportunity."

- Configure Trigger ➤ A record is created or updated.

- Set Entry Conditions ➤ Condition Requirements ➤ Custom Condition Logic is Met.

- Field ➤ StageName.

- Operator ➤ Equal.

- Value ➤ Negotiation/Review.

- Click Save button on the top right.

Step 3: Put the Flow Label in the field. Flow API Name will be automatically populated. Click Save button.

Save the flow

* Flow Label

Opportunity review

* Flow API Name

Opportunity_review

Description

Show Advanced

Cancel   Save

Step 4: Now click + to add the new element on the canvas. Click Set Records.

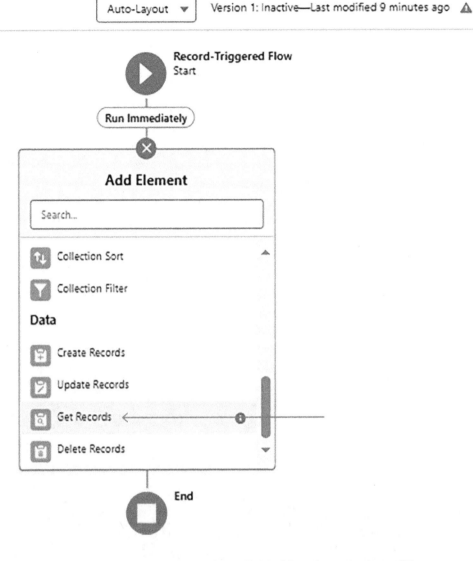

Step 5: Put the name Opportunity ID in the Lebel field and API Name will be automatically populated.

Note! Try to consistently name conditions across all elements. This naming convention has a significant impact on the automatic generation of API names for these elements. The importance of this approach will become apparent in the next steps when utilizing API names in the building processes of other elements:

- Get Records of This Object ➤ Object ➤ Opportunity

- Filter Opportunity Records ➤ Field ➤ ID

- Filter Opportunity Records ➤ Operator ➤ Equals

- Filter Opportunity Records ➤ Value ➤ $Records ➤ Opportunity ID

Version 1: Inactive—Last modified an hour ago ⚠ | Run | Debug | View Tests | Activate | Save As | **Save**

New Get Records

* Label
`Opportunity_ID` ◀

* API Name
`Opportunity_ID`

Description

Get Records of This Object

* Object
`Opportunity`

Filter Opportunity Records

Condition Requirements
`Custom Condition Logic Is Met ▼`

* Condition Logic ℹ
`1`

	Field	Operator	Value	
1	Id	Equals ▼	Aₐ $Record > Opportunity ID ✕	🗑

+ Add Condition

Sort Opportunity Records

Sort Order
`Ascending ▼`

* Sort By
`StageName`

How Many Records to Store
- ⦿ Only the first record
- ◯ All records

How to Store Record Data
- ⦿ Automatically store all fields
- ◯ Choose fields and let Salesforce do the rest
- ◯ Choose fields and assign variables (advanced)

Step 6: Now click + to add the new element on the canvas. Click Action.

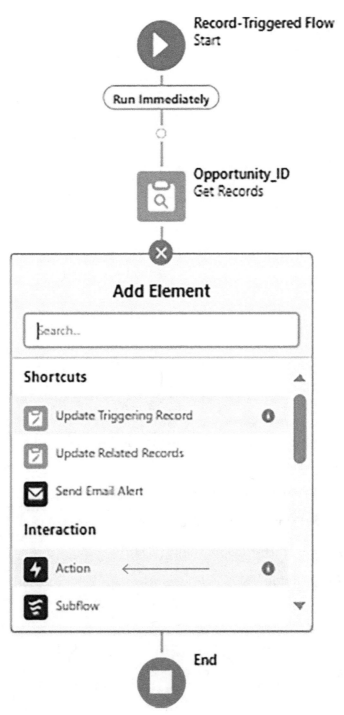

Step 7: Type in the search field "Chatter" and choose Post to Chatter.

Step 8: Put the name Chatter_Message in the Label field, and API Name will be automatically populated.

- Set Input Values for Selected Action

- Message ➤ {!Opportunity_ID.Name}

- Target Name or ID ➤ {!Opportunity_ID.Id}

- Click Done Button

Edit Post to Chatter

Use values from earlier in the flow to set the inputs for the "Post to Chatter" core action. To use its outputs later in the flow, store them in variables.

Chatter_Message (Chatter_Message) ✎

Set Input Values for the Selected Action

A_a * Message ⓘ

> {!Opportunity_ID.Name}   ←————

A_a * Target Name or ID   ⓘ

> {!Opportunity_ID.Id}   ←————

A_a Experience Cloud Site ID

⬤ Don't Include

☰ Target Type

⬤ Don't Include

☰ Visibility

⬤ Don't Include

> Advanced

Cancel   Done

Step 9: Now click + to add the new element on the canvas. Click Create Records.

Step 10: Put the name Account_Task in the Lebel field and API Name will be automatically populated.

- How Many Records to Create ➤ One

- How to Set the Records Fields ➤ Use separate resources and literal values

- Create a Record of This Object Object ➤ Task

- Set Field Values for the Task ➤ Field ➤ Subject ➤ Call

- Set Field Values for the Task ➤ Field ➤ Whatid ➤ Opportunity from Opportunity_ID ➤ Account ID ➤ Account ID

- Set Field Values for the Task ➤ Field ➤ Description ➤ Opportunity from Opportunity_ID ➤ Stage

- Click on Save As Button

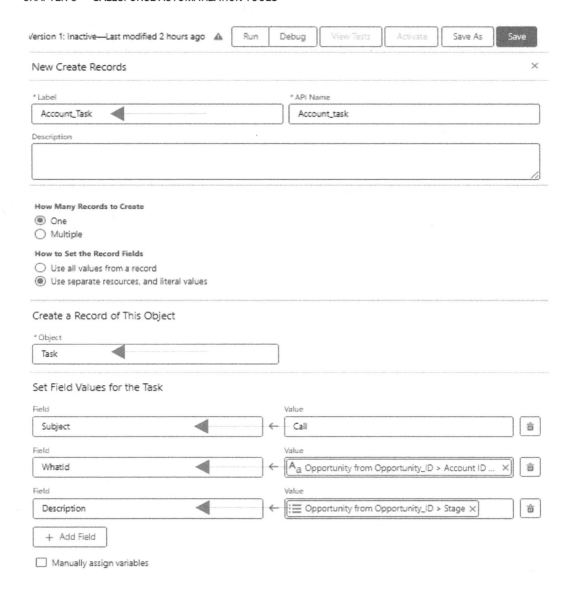

- Field ➤ Flow Label ➤ Type "Opportunity review"
- Click on Save button and save a new created Flow.

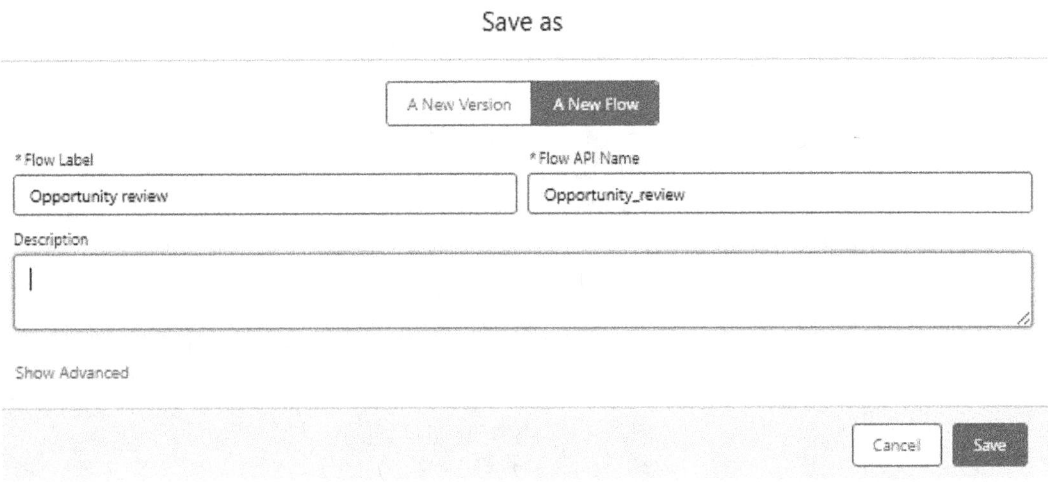

Save as

| A New Version | A New Flow |

* Flow Label

Opportunity review

* Flow API Name

Opportunity_review

Description

Show Advanced

Cancel   Save

- Your Flow is created as below.

- Click on Activate button on the top to activate the Flow within your Salesforce org.

- Check the newly created Flow by building a new Opportunity and changing the Stage to Negotiation/Review.

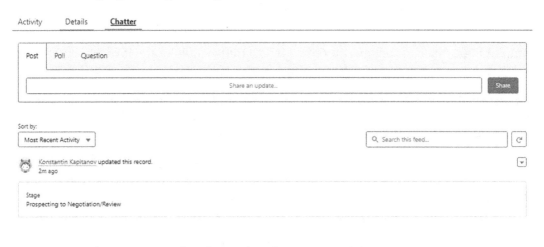

- See the new created task on related account activity.

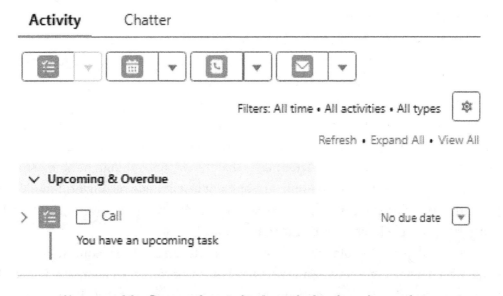

3.6 Invocable Methods in Flows

Invocable methods in Salesforce allow developers to expose Apex methods as custom actions in the Flow Builder. These custom actions can be used in flows to perform complex logic that cannot be achieved with declarative tools alone. Invocable methods can receive input parameters from flows, perform some processing, and return output values. The input and output parameters can be of primitive data types, sObjects, or collections of these data types.

To use an invocable method in a flow, you must first create the method in Apex with the **@InvocableMethod** annotation.

The input and output parameters must be declared as public or global, and must be of the supported data types. Further, the parameters need to be accessible, they should specifically be annotated with @InvocableVariable. Once the method is created, it can be selected as an Apex action in the Flow Builder.

In a flow, the Apex action can be added to the canvas and configured with input parameters. These input parameters can be derived from variables or values obtained from other elements in the flow, such as record lookups or user inputs. When the flow runs, the Apex action is executed with the specified input parameters, and returns output values that can be used in subsequent flow elements.

Considerations when Using Invocable Methods in Flows

When using invocable methods in flows, there are some considerations to keep in mind. First, invocable methods should be designed to be bulkified, as flows can process multiple records at once. This means that the methods should be able to handle collections of input and output parameters, and not just a single record. Additionally, the input and output parameters should be of supported data types, as flows are bulkified and can run multiple interviews in one transaction.

It is also important to note that invocable methods run in system context by default, which means that the sharing rules and record-level access are not enforced. This can be a security risk if the method is used to modify or access sensitive data. It is recommended to use invocable methods only for non-sensitive operations, or to add appropriate security checks in the method implementation.

Overall, invocable methods provide a powerful way to extend the capabilities of Salesforce flows and perform complex logic using Apex. By designing the methods to be bulkified and using supported data types, developers can create reusable and efficient solutions that can be easily maintained.

Let's add an action to our created flow, where @InvocableMethod is used to encapsulate custom logic that updates opportunity fields. This could be useful if the logic involves complex calculations, updates to multiple fields, or other operations that are better handled in Apex code. The flow triggers this logic after creating the task when the opportunity reaches the Negotiation/Review stage. We will set Close Date to three days from the current date for opportunities that have reached the Negotiation/Review stage. This ensures that the Close Date is updated only for opportunities in the specified stage.

Step 1: We need to create new Apex class "OpportunityUpdater" including @InvocableMethod as follows. Use the Developer Console menu ➤ File ➤ New ➤ Apex Class, see more information in the next chapter.

```
public class OpportunityUpdater {
    public class OpportunityUpdateInput {
        @InvocableVariable(label='Opportunity Id' required=true)
        public Id opportunityId;
    }

    @InvocableMethod(label='Update Opportunity Fields'
    description='Updates opportunity fields based on custom logic')
    public static void updateOpportunityFields
    (List<OpportunityUpdateInput> inputList) {
        // Implement your custom logic here (if needed)
        // You can access the opportunityId from each input and
        // perform the necessary updates

        List<Opportunity> opportunitiesToUpdate = new List<Opportunity>();

        // Retrieve opportunities with the 'Negotiation/Review' stage

        List<Opportunity> negotiationReviewOpportunities = [SELECT
        Id, StageName, CloseDate FROM Opportunity WHERE StageName =
        'Negotiation/Review'];

        for (Opportunity oppToUpdate : negotiationReviewOpportunities) {
            // Set Close Date to three days from today
            oppToUpdate.CloseDate = Date.today().addDays(3);
            opportunitiesToUpdate.add(oppToUpdate);
        }
```

```
    // Update the opportunities
    if (!opportunitiesToUpdate.isEmpty()) {
        update opportunitiesToUpdate;
    }
  }
}
```

The provided Apex code represents a class called "OpportunityUpdater" with a nested class called "OpportunityUpdateInput" and a static method called "updateOpportunityFields." The code is designed to update the CloseDate field of opportunities with the StageName set to "Negotiation/Review" to three days from the current date.

The "OpportunityUpdateInput" class has a single member variable, "opportunityId," of type Id. This variable is marked with the "@InvocableVariable" annotation, indicating that it is an input variable for an invocable method.

The "updateOpportunityFields" method takes a list of "OpportunityUpdateInput" objects as input. Inside the method, a query is used to retrieve a list of opportunities with the StageName set to "Negotiation/Review." The CloseDate field of each opportunity is then updated to three days from the current date. The updated opportunities are added to a list called "opportunitiesToUpdate." Finally, if the "opportunitiesToUpdate" list is not empty, the opportunities are updated using the "update" keyword.

Step 2: Now open new created "Opportunity review" Flow and click + to add the new action to our created flow after Opportunity_ID element on the canvas.

Step 3: Choose Type on the left menu.

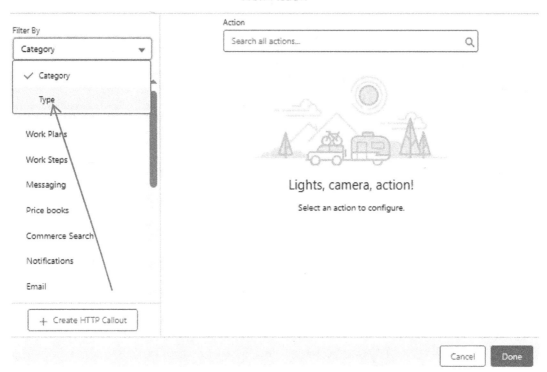

Step 4: Choose Apex Action ➤ Update Opportunity Fields.

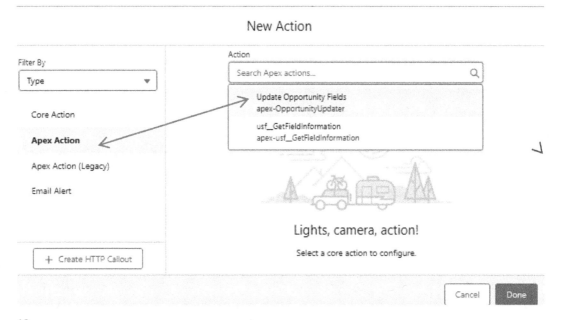

Step 5: Put the name New update in the Label field, and API Name will be automatically populated.

- Opportunity Id field ➤ {!Opportunity_ID.Id}

New Action

Filter By	Action
Type ▼	Update Opportunity Fields

Core Action

Apex Action

Apex Action (Legacy)

Email Alert

Use values from earlier in the flow to set the inputs for the "Update Opportunity Fields" Apex action. To use its outputs later in the flow, store them in variables.

* Label	* API Name
New Update	New_Update

Description

Set Input Values for the Selected Action

A_a * Opportunity Id 🛈

{!Opportunity_ID.Id}

+ Create HTTP Callout

Cancel   Done

Step 6: Your Flow is updated as below.

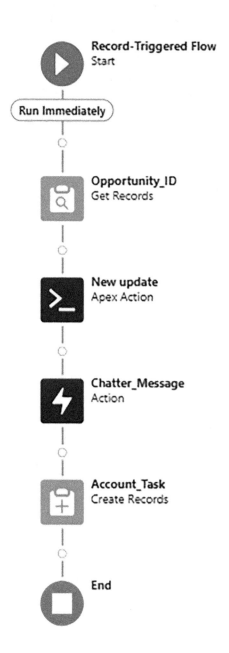

- Save your updated Flow and ensure that it is activated.

- Check the updated Flow by building a new Opportunity and changing the Stage to Negotiation/Review.

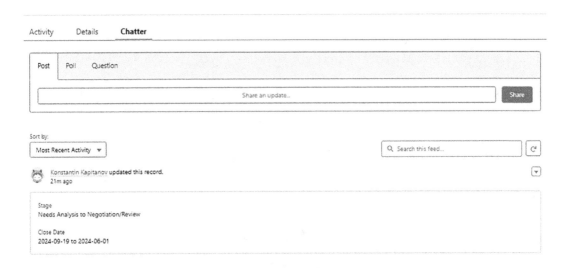

- See the updated Close Date of the related Opportunity.

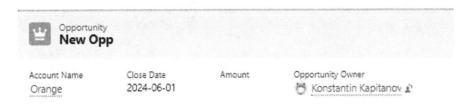

CHAPTER 4

Apex Programming

4.1 Apex Programming Language Syntax

Apex is a programming language developed by Salesforce specifically for building applications on the Salesforce platform. It shares similarities with Java in terms of syntax and structure, as it's influenced by Java. It is a strongly typed, case-insensitive, object-oriented language. As operate on multi-tenant environment, you can save your code against different API versions. Apex is integrated with the database, which means it can access and manipulate records without the need to establish the database connection explicitly. You can write custom business logic by creating triggers and classes. Triggers are pieces of code that automatically execute when certain events occur, such as the insertion, update, or deletion of records. Apex classes can encapsulate complex logic that can be reused across multiple parts of your application. Apex supports single-line comments (//) and multi-line comments (/* */) to add explanatory notes or disable code temporarily.

```
// This is a single-line comment in Apex
Integer myInt = 5; // This is another single-line comment

/*
This is a multi-line comment in Apex
It can span multiple lines and is useful for commenting out large
blocks of code
Integer myInt = 5;
String myString = 'Hello, world!';
*/
```

© Konstantin Kapitanov 2024
K. Kapitanov, *Salesforce Developer I Certification*, Certification Study Companion Series,
https://doi.org/10.1007/979-8-8688-0300-0_4

Batch processing is supported, which allows you to efficiently process large volumes of data in chunks, reducing the impact on system performance. Governor limits enforces on Apex code ensure efficient and fair use of the platform's resources. Salesforce provides tools for debugging and logging Apex code, making it easier to identify and rectify issues in your applications.

4.2 Anonymous Window in Developer Console

The Developer Console is a powerful tool that allows you to write and execute Apex code, including anonymous Apex, which is a way to run code snippets without saving them to the metadata.

Here's how you can use the Developer Console to execute Apex code anonymously:

1. *Open the Developer Console*: In Salesforce, click your name on the top-right corner, and then select "Developer Console" from the dropdown menu.

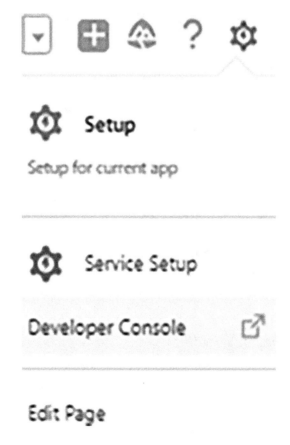

2. *Open the Execute Anonymous Window*: In the Developer Console, click on the "Debug" menu at the top, and then select "Open Execute Anonymous Window".

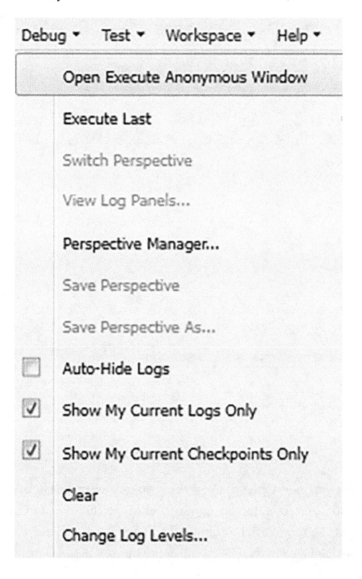

3. *Write Your Apex Code*: In the "Enter Apex Code" window that appears, you can write your Apex code snippet. This code can be any valid Apex code, such as a class, method, or a single line of code.

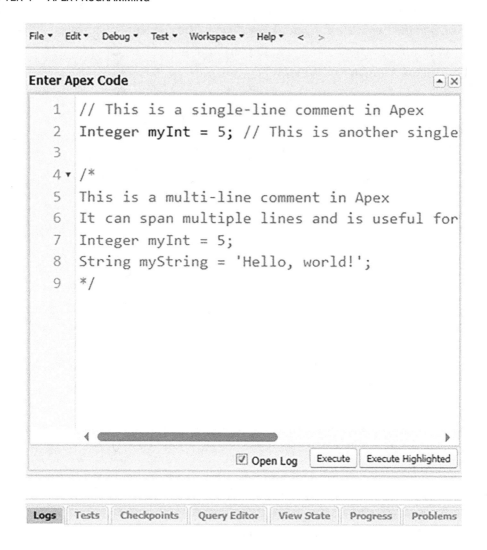

4.   *Execute the Code*: Once you've written your Apex code, click the "Execute" button at the top-right corner of the "Enter Apex Code" window. The code will be compiled and executed, and the results will be displayed in the "Logs" tab at the bottom of the Developer Console.

5.   *View the Results*: After executing the code, you can view the results in the "Logs" tab. The logs will show any debug statements or error messages generated by your code.

Executing Apex Execute Anonymous can be useful for a variety of reasons, including

- *Quick Testing*: The Execute Anonymous feature allows you to quickly test small snippets of Apex code without the need to create a separate class or trigger. This can be useful for experimenting with code, checking the behavior of specific methods, or verifying the results of a particular logic.

- *Data Manipulation*: You can use Execute Anonymous to perform data manipulation tasks, such as inserting, updating, or deleting records in your Salesforce org. This can be helpful when you need to make changes to your data without going through the process of creating a custom Apex class or trigger.

- *Debugging*: Execute Anonymous can be used for debugging purposes. You can insert debug statements in your code, and execute it to check the values of variables, identify issues, or understand the flow of execution. This can be particularly useful when troubleshooting complex issues or understanding the behavior of existing code.

- *Quick Fixes*: Execute Anonymous is often used for one-time operations that don't require a permanent solution. For example, you might use it to perform a data migration, execute a batch job, or run a specific piece of code to address a temporary requirement.

It's important to keep in mind that Anonymous Blocks always run with sharing and can fail to run if the code violates the user's object- and field-level permissions.

4.3 Variables Data Types

As the data types of variables in Apex are generally strongly typed, you must declare the data type when you declare a variable. Declaring a variable means defining a container for holding data. When you declare a variable, you are essentially creating a named storage location in the computer's memory. In Apex, you can declare a variable like this:

```
DataType variableName;
```

Here, DataType represents the type of data the variable can hold, such as Integer, String, Boolean, etc., and variableName is the name you give to the variable. Assigning a value to a variable means storing a specific piece of data, of the appropriate data type, into the variable.

If you do not assign a value to a variable in Apex, it defaults to *null*. It essentially means the variable is empty or undefined. Apex starting calculations from 0, it's important to note that *null* is not the same as 0. *Null* means the variable has no value assigned to it, whereas 0 is a specific numerical value.

Data types define the kind of values that variables can hold. Data types help ensure that values are stored and processed correctly in your code. Apex supports several types of data, including primitive data types, collections, and special types for working with Salesforce records.

You can test the following provided code examples for the variables in Apex Anonymous Window. Setup ➤ Developer Console ➤ in Developer Console go to menu Debug ➤ Open Execute Anonymous Window put the code block and press on Execute button.

Primitive data types represent basic values including

Integer: A 32-bit number that does not contain any decimal points. Its value ranges between -2,147,483,648 and 2,147,483,647.

```
Integer myNumber;
myNumber = 5;
System.debug( myNumber);
```

Long: 64-bit number without any decimal point used when a range of values greater than an integer. It has a minimum value of -2^{63} and a maximum value of $2^{63}-1$.

```
Long myLongNumber;
myLongNumber = 1234567890L;
System.debug( myLongNumber);
```

Decimal: A decimal number 32-bit number with a decimal point. Decimal is used as default type by currency fields for financial calculations because it provides more precision than Double.

```
Decimal myDecimalNumber;
myDecimalNumber = 123.45;
System.debug( myDecimalNumber);
```

Double: A 64-bit number that can contain decimal points. Used for very large numbers which can include a decimal, with minimum value of -2^63 and a maximum value of 2^63-1.

```
Double myDoubleNumber;
myDoubleNumber = 3.14159;
System.debug( myDoubleNumber);
```

Boolean: Represents true or false values. You can use Boolean variables in conditional statements and logical operations to control the flow of your Apex code. Boolean variables are fundamental in programming and are commonly used for decision-making in various contexts within your code.

```
Boolean isTrue;
isTrue = true;

if (isTrue) {
    // Code to be executed if isTrue is true
}
else {
    // Code to be executed if isTrue is false
}
System.debug( istrue);
```

String: Textual data type used to store sequences of characters, such as text or words.

```
String myString;
myString = 'Hello, World!';
System.debug( myString);
```

You can manipulate strings in various ways, such as concatenation, substring extraction, and searching for specific characters or patterns.

Date: Represents a date value.

```
Date myDate;
myDate = Date.today();
System.debug( myDate);
```

You can perform various operations with date variables in Apex, such as comparing dates, calculating the difference between dates, and formatting dates into strings for display purposes.

Datetime: Represents a date and time. The myDatetime variable will hold the current date and time in the format "yyyy-MM-dd HH:mm:ss.SSSZ".

```
Datetime myDatetime;
myDatetime = Datetime.now();
System.debug( myDatetime);
```

Blob: A collection of binary data including images, files, or any other type of data that is not text-based, stored as a single object.

```
Blob myBlob;
// Create an empty Blob
Blob emptyBlob = Blob.valueOf('');
System.debug(myBlob);
```

Remember the difference between *null* or 0 as we discussed at the beginning of the chapter.

ID: As alphanumeric identifier is set to a 15-character value but Apex automatically converts it to the corresponding 18-character ID.

```
ID MyID = '001xx000003DGbKAAW';
System.debug(MyID);
```

Object: The main purpose of using the Object variable in Apex is to provide a generic type that can hold any type of object. It allows for flexibility in handling different data types without specifying a specific type upfront. This variable is useful for casting operations and scenarios where you need a generic type that can hold any object.

```
// Assign an Integer to an Object variable
Object obj = 42;

// Cast the Object variable to an Integer and perform operations
Integer num = (Integer)obj;
Integer square = num * num;

System.debug('Number: ' + num);
System.debug('Square: ' + square);
```

SObject: In Apex, the sObject is a fundamental data type that represents an object in Salesforce's data mode in connection with metadata. It's a generic type used to work with records of any standard or custom object in the Salesforce database. An sObject is a data type in Salesforce Apex that represents a row of data and can only be declared using the SOAP API name of the object. Every Salesforce record is natively represented as an sObject in Apex. SObjects are used to hold record information in the Force.com database. Developers refer to sObjects and their fields by their API names. The standard objects have typically more standardized system predefined API names to use:

```
Lead myLead = new Lead();
myLead.FirstName = 'Max';
myLead.LastName = 'James';
System.debug(myLead);
```

The API name for custom objects is based on the object's API name when it was created. For example, if you create a custom object named "Project," its API name might be Project__C.

It's important to note that API names for custom objects and fields are often suffixed with __c, while standard objects and fields typically do not have this suffix.

For standard fields, the API name usually combines the object's API name with the field's API name, and for custom fields separated by double underscores. For example:

Standard Field on Lead: API Name: Lead.LastName

Custom Field on Account: API Name: Account.CustomerPriority__c

Additionally, you need to ensure that the field is accessible and visible to the user or context in which your Apex code is executing.

Enum: An enum in Salesforce Apex is an abstract data type that allows you to define a set of values that an identifier can take on. Each value in the enum is given a unique identifier, and you can use these identifiers to reference the values in your code. Enums are used to define a predefined set of values that a variable can take, making your code more readable and maintainable. Enums are often used to represent specific values within your Apex code.

Here's an example of how you might define and use an enum in Salesforce Apex:

```
public enum Season {
    WINTER, SPRING, SUMMER, FALL
}
Season currentSeason = Season.SUMMER;
System.debug('The current season is ' + currentSeason);
```

You cannot change the data type of a variable after it has been defined. However, you can perform type casting and data type conversion operations.

Casting in Apex refers to the process of converting one data type to another. It allows you to treat an object as an instance of a different class or to convert a primitive data type to another primitive data type. Casting is useful when you need to perform operations or assignments that require a specific data type.

Explicit converting is when you manually convert one data type to another. It is used when there is a possibility of data loss or when you want to be explicit about the conversion.

Here's an example of explicit conversion in Apex:

```
Double decimalNum = 10.53;
Integer intValue = (Integer) decimalNum;
System.debug( intValue);
```

In the example above, we explicitly convert the Double variable *decimalNum* to an Integer. This allows us to assign the value of decimalNum to intValue, but note that there may be a loss of precision.

Implicit converting, also known as automatic converting, is when the conversion happens automatically without the need for explicit syntax. It occurs when there is no possibility of data loss or when the conversion is well-defined.

Here's an example of implicit converting in Apex:

```
Integer num = 10;
Long bigNum = num;
System.debug (num);
```

In the example above, we assign the value of the Integer variable num to the Long variable bigNum without explicitly converting it. This is possible because there is no loss of precision when converting from Integer to Long.

Converting from Integer to String:

```
Integer myInteger = 42;
String myString = String.valueOf(myInteger);
// Explicit converting from Integer to String
System.debug(myInteger);
```

Converting from String to Integer:

```
String myString = '42';
Integer myInteger = Integer.valueOf(myString);
// Explicit converting from String to Integer
System.debug(myString);
```

In general, variables should be declared outside of curly braces if they need to be accessible outside of the block in which they are declared.

```
Integer outsideVariable = 5;
System.debug(outsideVariable); // Valid
```

However, there may be cases where it makes sense to declare variables inside curly braces, such as when you want to limit the scope of a variable to a specific block of code. Variables declared inside curly braces have limited visibility, known as block scope. They are only accessible within the specific set of curly braces where they are defined.

```
{
    Integer insideVariable = 10;
    System.debug(insideVariable); // Valid
}
System.debug(insideVariable);
// Error: Variable does not exist: insideVariable
```

In Apex programming, the terminology of "casting" can be used in different contexts. Upcasting and downcasting refer to the conversion of object references between classes that are related through inheritance. Upcasting involves treating an object as an instance of its superclass, while downcasting involves treating an object as an instance of its subclass. On the other hand, casting of primitive data types involves converting primitive data types to other primitive data types, as demonstrated in our examples.

4.4 Collections

In Apex, collections are data structures used to store and manage multiple values of the same or different data types. Collections allow you to work with groups of related data in a more organized and efficient way compared to using individual variables. There are three main types of collections in Apex: Lists, Sets, and Maps.

Lists: List elements can be of any data type, including primitive types, collections, and custom data types. They can dynamically resize themselves, meaning you can add or remove elements from a list without specifying its size beforehand. Lists in Apex are typed, which means you specify the type of elements the list will hold. For example, you can have a list of integers, strings, objects, and another. Elements in a list are accessed by their index, starting from 0. For example, the first element in a list is accessed using index 0, the second element using index 1, and so on. Some of the most common methods used while interacting with a list include

- *add()*: Adds an element to the end of the list

- *get()*: Returns the element at the specified index

- *remove()*: Removes the element at the specified index

- *size()*: Returns the number of elements in the list

- *sort()*: Sorts the elements in the list in ascending order

When you add elements to the list using the add() method, the list grows in size. For example, if you add three elements (A, B, and C) to the list, your line now has these elements positioned along it: | A | B | C |

You can remove elements from the list using methods like remove(). If you remove element B, the line looks like this: | A | C |

This Apex code creates a list of strings called names, adds three strings ("Alice," "Bob," and "Charlie") to the list, and then prints the second string ("Bob") to the system log using System.debug().

```
List<String> names = new List<String>();
names.add('Alice');
names.add('Bob');
names.add('Charlie');
System.debug(names[1]);
```

Execution Log		
Timestamp	Event	Details
11:45:22:002	USER_DEBUG	[5]|DEBUG|Bob

Here's another example of using a list to store and manipulate names:

```
List<String> names = new List<String>();
names.add('Alice');
names.add('Bob');
names.add('Charlie');
System.debug(names[1]);
names.remove(0);
for (String name : names) {
    System.debug(name);}
```

Execution Log		
Timestamp	Event	Details
11:50:16:022	USER_DEBUG	[5]|DEBUG|Bob
11:50:16:022	USER_DEBUG	[8]|DEBUG|Bob
11:50:16:022	USER_DEBUG	[8]|DEBUG|Charlie

Remove the first element ("Alice") from the list using names.remove(0); then iterate through the modified list (after removing "Alice"), printing each element ("Bob" and "Charlie") to the system log using a for loop and System.debug(name).

In the third example, we use another method with numbers:

```
List<Integer> numbers = new List<Integer>();

// Add elements to the list
numbers.add(5);
numbers.add(2);
numbers.add(8);
numbers.add(1);

// Get the number of elements in the list
Integer size = numbers.size();
System.debug('Size of the list: ' + size);
// Output: Size of the list: 4

// Access elements in the list
Integer firstNumber = numbers.get(0);
System.debug('First number: ' + firstNumber);
// Output: First number: 5
```

```
// Sort the elements in the list
numbers.sort();
System.debug('Sorted list: ' + numbers);
// Output: Sorted list: (1, 2, 5, 8)
```

In this example, we create a list called numbers and add some integer values to it. We then use the size() method to get the number of elements in the list, and the get() method to access the element at index 0 (the first element in the list). Finally, we use the sort() method to sort the elements in ascending order.

Sets: A set is an unordered collection of unique elements. Sets are useful when you want to ensure that there are no duplicate values in your collection. Sets only contain unique elements. If you attempt to add a duplicate element to a Set, the Set will ignore the duplicate value. Unlike Lists, Sets do not have indices. You cannot directly access elements in a Set using an index because Sets are unordered collections. Sets are commonly used when you want to store a collection of unique values, perform set operations, or check for the presence of specific elements in a collection without caring about the order in which they were added. Some commonly used methods to manipulate sets include

- *add()*: Adds an element to the set.
- *remove()*: Removes an element from the set.
- *contains()*: Checks if a specific element is present in the set.
- *addAll()*: Adds all elements from another set to the current set.
- *retainAll()*: Retains only the elements that are present in both sets.
- *removeAll()*: Removes all elements that are present in another set from the current set.
- *size()*: Returns the number of elements in the set.
- *isEmpty()*: Checks if the set is empty.
- *clear()*: Removes all elements from the set.

An example is shown as follows.

```
Set<Integer> numbers = new Set<Integer>();
numbers.add(5);
numbers.add(10);
numbers.add(5);
System.debug(numbers);
```

Execution Log		
Timestamp	Event	Details
12:01:39:002	USER_DEBUG	[5]|DEBUG|{5, 10}

Add two integers, 5 and 10, to the numbers set. Sets do not allow duplicate elements, so the duplicate 5 is ignored. Print the contents of the numbers set, displaying [5, 10] to the system log using System.debug(numbers).

The following is an another example to use a Set to gather all the unique email addresses from a list of contacts:

```
List<Contact> contacts = [SELECT Email FROM Contact];
Set<String> uniqueEmails = new Set<String>();
for (Contact contact : contacts) {
    uniqueEmails.add(contact.Email); }
System.debug('Unique Email Addresses: ' + uniqueEmails);
```

In this example, the uniqueEmails Set ensures that only distinct email addresses are added, eliminating any duplicates.

We can also use additional methods with names.

```
Set<String> fruits = new Set<String>();

// Add elements to the set
fruits.add('Apple');
fruits.add('Banana');
fruits.add('Mango');

// Get the number of elements in the set
Integer size = fruits.size();
System.debug('Size of the set: ' + size);
// Output: Size of the set: 3

// Check if the set is empty
Boolean isEmpty = fruits.isEmpty();
System.debug('Is the set empty? ' + isEmpty);
// Output: Is the set empty? false
```

```
// Check if the set contains a specific element
Boolean containsBanana = fruits.contains('Banana');
System.debug('Does the set contain Banana? ' + containsBanana);
// Output: Does the set contain Banana? true

// Remove an element from the set
fruits.remove('Banana');
System.debug('Updated set: ' + fruits);
// Output: Updated set:{Apple, Mango}

// Clear all elements from the set
fruits.clear();
System.debug('Cleared set: ' + fruits);
// Output: Cleared set: {}

// Create another set
Set<String> moreFruits = new Set<String>{'Orange', 'Grapes'};

// Add all elements from another set
fruits.addAll(moreFruits);
System.debug('Combined set: ' + fruits);
// Output: Combined set: {Orange, Grapes}

// Iterate over elements in the set
for (String fruit : fruits) {
    System.debug('Fruit: ' + fruit);
}
```

Maps: A map is a collection of key-value pairs, where each key is unique and maps to a corresponding value. Maps are often used to associate related data. Maps are useful when you want to associate related pieces of information and quickly retrieve the value associated with a specific key. The key and value in a Map can be of any data type: primitive types, sObjects, user-defined objects, and another. Apex provides various methods to manipulate maps. Some commonly used methods include

- *put()*: Adds or updates an element in the map

- *get()*: Returns the value associated with a specific key

- *containsKey()*: Checks if a specific key is present in the map

- *remove()*: Removes an element from the map

- *keySet()*: Returns a set of all keys in the map

- *values()*: Returns a list of all values in the map

For example:

```
Map<String, Integer> ageMap = new Map<String, Integer>();
ageMap.put('Alice', 25);
ageMap.put('Bob', 30);
System.debug(ageMap.get('Alice'));
```

Initialize an empty map named ageMap to store string keys (names) and their corresponding integer values (ages). Add two key-value pairs to the ageMap like Alice and Bob. Retrieve the value associated with the key "Alice" from the ageMap using ageMap.get("Alice"), and print the retrieved value (25) to the system log using System.debug(ageMap.get('Alice')).

As another example, you might use a Map to associate account names with their corresponding balances. In this example, the Map allows you to quickly retrieve the balance associated with a specific account name.

```
Map<String, Decimal> accountBalances = new Map<String, Decimal>();
accountBalances.put('Acct1', 1000.00);
accountBalances.put('Acct2', 2500.00);
Decimal balance = accountBalances.get('Acct1');
System.debug('Balance of Acct1: ' + balance);
```

Here's an example that demonstrates the commonly used methods containsKey(), remove(), keySet(), and values() for manipulating maps in Apex:

```
Map<String, Integer> studentMarks = new Map<String, Integer>();

// Add key-value pairs to the map
studentMarks.put('John', 80);
studentMarks.put('Emily', 95);
studentMarks.put('Michael', 75);

// Check if the map contains a specific key
Boolean containsJohn = studentMarks.containsKey('John');
System.debug('Does the map contain John? ' + containsJohn);
// Output: Does the map contain John? true
```

69

```
// Remove a key-value pair from the map
studentMarks.remove('Michael');
System.debug('Updated map: ' + studentMarks);
// Output: Updated map: {John=80, Emily=95}

// Get a set of all keys in the map
Set<String> keys = studentMarks.keySet();
System.debug('Keys in the map: ' + keys);
// Output: Keys in the map: {John, Emily}

// Get a list of all values in the map
List<Integer> values = studentMarks.values();
System.debug('Values in the map: ' + values);
// Output: Values in the map: (80, 95)
```

In this example, we have a map called studentMarks that stores the marks of different students. We use the put() method to add key-value pairs to the map, where the key represents the student's name and the value represents the student's marks.

We then demonstrate the usage of the containsKey() method to check if the map contains a specific key ("John" in this case).

Next, we use the remove() method to remove a key-value pair from the map, in this case, the entry for "Michael."

We also demonstrate the keySet() method, which returns a set of all keys in the map, and the values() method, which returns a list of all values in the map.

Finally, we print the keys and values to verify the contents of the map.

4.5 Operators and Control Statements

Salesforce Apex provides a variety of operators that you can use to perform different operations on variables or values. These operators include arithmetic operators, comparison operators, logical operators, assignment operators, and more. Let's go through each type of operator:

Arithmetic Operators

Addition (+): Adds two values together.

```
Integer a = 5;
Integer b = 3;
Integer sum = a + b;
System.debug('Sum of a and b: ' + sum);
// Output: Sum of a and b: 8
```

Subtraction (-): Subtracts one value from another.

```
Integer a = 5;
Integer b = 3;
Integer difference = a - b; // Subtracting 'b' from 'a'
System.debug('Difference between a and b: ' + difference);
```

Multiplication (*): Multiplies two values together.

```
Integer a = 5;
Integer b = 3;
Integer product = a * b; // Multiplying 'a' and 'b'
System.debug('Product of a and b: ' + product);
```

Division (/): Divides one value by another.

```
Integer a = 10;
Integer b = 2;
Decimal quotient = (Decimal) a / b; // Dividing 'a' by 'b'
System.debug('Quotient of a and b: ' + quotient);
```

Increment (++) and Decrement (--): Increases or decreases the value of a variable by 1.

```
Integer count = 5;
count++; // Equivalent to: count = count + 1;
System.debug('Updated count: ' + count);
// Output: Updated count: 6
```

Another example by decreasing the value.

```
Integer count = 8;
count--; // Equivalent to: count = count - 1;
System.debug('Updated count: ' + count);
// Output: Updated count: 7
```

Comparison Operators

Equality (==) and Inequality (!=): Checks if two values are equal or not as in two examples with integer and string type as follows:

```
Integer num1 = 5;
Integer num2 = 5;
Boolean areEqual = num1 == num2;
if (areEqual) {
    System.debug('num1 and num2 are equal.');
} else {
      System.debug('num1 and num2 are not equal.');
 }
```

Another example with string value.

```
String str1 = 'Hello';
String str2 = 'World';
Boolean areStringsNotEqual = str1 != str2;

if (areStringsNotEqual) {
    System.debug('str1 and str2 are not equal.');
} else {
    System.debug('str1 and str2 are equal.');
}
```

Greater than (>): Checks if one value is greater than another.

```
Integer num1 = 10;
Integer num2 = 5;

if (num1 > num2) {
    System.debug('num1 is greater than num2.');
} else {
```

```
    System.debug('num1 is not greater than num2.');
}
```

Less than (<): Checks if one value is less than another.

```
Integer num1 = 5;
Integer num2 = 10;

if (num1 < num2) {
    System.debug('num1 is less than num2.');
} else {
    System.debug('num1 is not less than num2.');
}
```

Greater than or equal to (>=): Checks if one value is greater than or equal to another.

```
Integer num1 = 10;
Integer num2 = 10;

if (num1 >= num2) {
    System.debug('num1 is greater than or equal to num2.');
} else {
    System.debug('num1 is less than num2.');
}
```

Less than or equal to (<=): Checks if one value is less than or equal to another.

```
Integer num1 = 5;
Integer num2 = 5;

if (num1 <= num2) {
    System.debug('num1 is less than or equal to num2.');
} else {
    System.debug('num1 is greater than num2.');
}
```

Logical Operators

AND (&&): Returns true if both conditions are true.

```
Boolean isRaining = true;
Boolean hasUmbrella = true;
if (isRaining && hasUmbrella) {
    System.debug('You can go out with an umbrella.');
} else {
 System.debug
 ('It\'s either not raining or you don\'t have an umbrella.');
}
```

OR (||): Returns true if at least one of the conditions is true.

```
Boolean hasPermission = true;
Boolean isAdmin = false;
if (hasPermission || isAdmin) {
    System.debug('You have permission to access.');
} else {
System.debug('You do not have permission to access.');
}
```

NOT (!): Returns the opposite boolean value of the condition.

```
Boolean hasPermission = false;
if (!hasPermission) {
    System.debug('You do not have permission to access.');
} else {
System.debug('You have permission to access.');
 }
```

Assignment Operators

Assign (=): Assigns a value to a variable.

```
Integer num1 = 5;
Integer num2;

num2 = num1;

System.debug('num1: ' + num1);
System.debug('num2: ' + num2);
```

Addition assignment (+=): Adds a value to the current value of a variable and assigns the result to the same variable.

```
Integer total = 10;
Integer increment = 5;
total += increment;
System.debug('Updated total: ' + total);
// Output: Updated total: 15
```

Subtraction assignment (-=): Subtracts a value from the current value of a variable and assigns the result to the same variable.

```
Integer total = 20;
Integer decrement = 8;
total -= decrement;
System.debug('Updated total: ' + total);
// Output: Updated total: 12
```

Multiplication assignment (*=): Multiplies the current value of a variable by a value and assigns the result to the same variable.

```
Integer base = 5;
Integer multiplier = 3;
base *= multiplier; // Equivalent to: base = base * multiplier;
System.debug('Result: ' + base); // Output: Result: 15
```

Division assignment (/=): Divides the current value of a variable by a value and assigns the result to the same variable.

```
Decimal dividend = 20.0;
Decimal divisor = 4.0;
dividend /= divisor; // Equivalent to: dividend = dividend /divisor;
System.debug('Result: ' + dividend); // Output: Result: 5.0
```

Control statements in Apex are used to control the flow of execution in a program. They enable you to make decisions, repeat actions, and execute different parts of code based on conditions. Here are some common control statements in Apex along with examples:

if Statement: The if statement is used to execute a block of code if a specified condition is true. It is a fundamental control structure in programming. It allows you to execute certain blocks of code based on whether a given condition is true or false. Let's dive into the details of how the if statement works. The basic syntax of an if statement is as follows:

```
Integer x = 10;
if (x > 5) {
    System.debug('x is greater than 5');
} else {
    System.debug('x is not greater than 5');
}
```

The if statement checks whether x is greater than 5. Since x is indeed 10, which is greater than 5, the condition evaluates to true.

As a result, the code inside the curly braces following the if statement is executed, and the debug message "x is greater than 5" is printed.

The else block is not executed since the if condition is satisfied.

If the value of x were less than or equal to 5, then the condition would be false, and the code within the else block would be executed.

Remember that the else block is optional. If you only want to execute code when the condition is true and do nothing when it's false, you can omit the else block altogether.

The if statement is the building block for more complex decision-making processes in programming. You can also nest multiple if statements inside each other, or use else if statements to handle multiple conditions. This allows you to create more intricate decision trees based on various conditions.

switch Statement: The switch statement is used to evaluate a variable or expression against multiple possible values and execute different code blocks based on the matched value. It provides a way to streamline multiple if and else if conditions when you have a specific value to check against. The switch statement is particularly useful when you have a set of discrete values you want to compare against a single variable. Here's an example using the switch statement in Apex:

```
String fruit = 'apple';

switch on fruit {
    when 'apple' {
        System.debug('You selected an apple.');
    }
    when 'banana' {
        System.debug('You selected a banana.');
    }
```

```
    when else {
        System.debug('You selected a different fruit.');
    }
}
```

In this example, the switch statement compares the value of the *fruit variable* against different cases. Since f*ruit is "apple,"* the first case is matched, and the corresponding message is printed. Keep in mind that the switch statement in Apex only works with equality comparisons. It cannot handle more complex conditions like comparisons using greater than or less than operators. If you need to evaluate conditions beyond simple equality, you would need to use an if statement or a combination of if and else if statements.

for Loop: The for loop is used to iterate over a range of values for a specified number of times. It is a procedural loop used to execute a block of code repeatedly for a predetermined number of iterations.

```
for (Integer i = 0; i < 10; i++) {
    System.debug('The value of i is: ' + i);
}
```

This loop will iterate 10 times, with the value of i starting at 0 and incrementing by 1 each time through the loop. The System.debug() statement will print the value of i to the debug log each time through the loop.

In this example, *i* is an integer variable that is used to keep track of the current iteration of the loop. The loop will continue to execute as long as i is less than 10. The *System.debug()* statement is just an example of code that could be executed inside the loop. Any valid Apex code could be used inside the loop to process data or perform other tasks.

Here's an another example using the for loop in Apex to iterate through a list of numbers:

```
List<Integer> numbers = new List<Integer>{1, 2, 3, 4, 5};

for (Integer num : numbers) {
    System.debug('Number: ' + num);
}
```

In this example:

- numbers is a list containing integers from 1 to 5.

- The for loop iterates over each element in the numbers list.

- The loop variable num is initialized with the value of each element in the list during each iteration.

- The code inside the loop body prints the value of num.

The output of this code would be

```
Number: 1
Number: 2
Number: 3
Number: 4
Number: 5
```

The for loop is particularly useful when you know the number of iterations you need to perform or when you're iterating over a specific sequence of values. If you don't know the exact number of iterations or you need to dynamically determine when to stop, you might want to use a while loop instead.

while Loop: The while loop as a procedural loop repeatedly executes a block of code as long as a specified condition is true. Unlike the for loop, which is often used when you know the number of iterations in advance, the while loop is useful when you want to continue looping until a specific condition is no longer met. Here's how the while loop works in Apex:

```
Integer count = 2;
while (count <= 6) {
    System.debug('Number: ' + count);
    count += 2;
}
```

In this example:

- The loop starts with the count variable initialized to 2.

- The while loop continues to execute as long as the condition count <= 6 is true.

- In each iteration, the loop prints the current value of count and then increments it by 2.

- Once count becomes 6, the condition count <= 6 becomes false, and the loop terminates.

The output of this code would be

```
Number: 2
Number: 4
Number: 6
```

It's important to ensure that the condition in a while loop eventually becomes false, or else you might end up in an infinite loop that never stops executing. To prevent this, make sure that the condition is being manipulated within the loop, such as by incrementing or decrementing a loop variable, so that it eventually changes and the loop terminates.

The choice between using a for loop and a while loop depends on the situation. If you know the number of iterations beforehand or have a specific sequence to iterate over, a for loop might be more appropriate. If you need to keep looping until a particular condition changes, a while loop is a better choice.

do-while Loop: The do-while procedural loop is similar to the while loop, but it executes the code block at least once, regardless of whether the condition is true or false. It's similar to the while loop, but with a key difference: the do-while loop always executes its block of code at least once before checking the loop condition. After the first execution, it then checks the condition and continues executing as long as the condition remains true.

Here's an example using the do-while loop in Apex to input a number from the user and ensure it's within a valid range:

```
Integer count = 1;
do {
    System.debug('Count: ' + count);
    count++;
} while (count <= 0);
```

In this example the initial value of count is 1, which is not less than or equal to 0. Therefore, the condition is false from the beginning, and the loop will not execute beyond the initial iteration.

The output of the code will be

```
Count: 1
```

Notice that the loop executes the code block at least once before checking the condition. This can be useful when you want to ensure that a certain piece of code runs before condition checking, regardless of whether the condition is initially met or not.

The do-while loop is particularly helpful when you need to ensure that an action is performed before condition evaluation, or when you want to guarantee at least one execution of a loop.

break Statement: The break statement is used to exit a loop prematurely. In a loop (such as a for, while, or do-while loop), the break statement is used to exit the loop prematurely. When a break statement is encountered within the loop's block of code, the program immediately exits the loop, and the subsequent iterations are not executed.

Example in a Loop:

```
// Declare and initialize a list of integers
List<Integer> numbers = new List<Integer>{1, 2, 3, 4, 5};

// Use a for loop to iterate over the list
for (Integer num : numbers) {
    if (num == 3) {
        break;
    }
    System.debug('Number: ' + num);
}
```

In this example, we have a list of integers called numbers which contains the values 1, 2, 3, 4, and 5. The for loop iterates over each element in the list and assigns it to the variable num. Inside the loop, we check if num is equal to 3 using the if statement. If it is, we use the break statement to exit out of the loop prematurely.

When you run this code, you will see the numbers 1 and 2 printed in the debug logs. The break statement is used to terminate the execution of a loop prematurely. In this case, when num is equal to 3, the loop is exited, and no further numbers are processed.

continue Statement: The continue statement is used to skip the rest of the current iteration and proceed to the next iteration of a loop. It's used when a certain condition is met, and you want to bypass the rest of the loop's code for the current iteration and move on to the next iteration.

In a loop (such as a for, while, or do-while loop), the continue statement is used to skip the remaining code within the current iteration and move to the next iteration of the loop.

```
for (Integer i = 1; i <= 5; i++) {
    if (i == 3) {
        continue;
    }
    System.debug('Current i: ' + i);
}
```

In this example, when i is 3, the continue statement is encountered. This causes the loop to skip the rest of the code within the current iteration and move directly to the next iteration. As a result, the output would be

```
Current i: 1
Current i: 2
Current i: 4
Current i: 5
```

The continue statement is particularly useful when you want to avoid executing certain code within a loop iteration based on a specific condition. It allows you to control the flow of the loop without prematurely exiting the entire loop, as would be the case with the break statement.

Remember that the continue statement should be used thoughtfully to ensure that your loop continues to behave as expected. Misusing it could lead to unexpected results or an infinite loop if used incorrectly.

CHAPTER 5

Data Manipulation Language (DML)

5.1 DML Statements and Operations

DML refers to the set of statements and operations that you can use to interact with records in the Salesforce database. DML operations are used to create, retrieve, update, and delete records in various Salesforce objects, such as custom and standard objects like accounts, contacts, opportunities, and more.

Salesforce provides a set of DML statements that you can use in your Apex code to perform these operations. You can execute these code examples one by one in the Anonymous Apex window. After running each example, you can check the results by opening the Account list in your Salesforce Sales Cloud and refreshing your browser.

Please note that executing DML operations in a production environment should be done with caution, especially when performing deletions. It's recommended to test such operations in a sandbox environment first to ensure the desired results.

Insert: Used to create new records in the database.

```
// Example List of Strings
List<String> fruitNames = new List<String>{'Apple', 'Banana',
'Orange', 'Grapes'};

// Create a list to store Account records
List<Account> fruitAccountsList = new List<Account>();

// Populate the list with Account records
for (String fruit : fruitNames) {
```

© Konstantin Kapitanov 2024
K. Kapitanov, *Salesforce Developer I Certification*, Certification Study Companion Series,
https://doi.org/10.1007/979-8-8688-0300-0_5

```
    Account newFruitAccount = new Account(Name=fruit);
    fruitAccountsList.add(newFruitAccount);
}

// Insert the Account records into the database
insert fruitAccountsList;

// Query the inserted records to verify
List<Account> insertedAccounts = [SELECT Id, Name FROM Account WHERE Name
IN :fruitNames];

// Iterate over the inserted records to verify
for (Account fruitAccount : insertedAccounts) {
    System.debug('Inserted Fruit Account: ' + + fruitAccount.Id + ' - ' +
    fruitAccount.Name);
}
```

In this example, we create a list (fruitAccountsList) to store Account records. We populate this list in a loop by creating Account instances for each fruit. Then, the insert statement is used to insert all the records in the fruitAccountsList into the Salesforce database. This includes generating a new unique ID for each Account object created in your loop. The Salesforce platform handles the generation of these IDs internally, and you don't need to explicitly manage or sign them yourself.

Upsert: Used to either update existing records or insert new records based on matching criteria.

```
// Example List of Strings
List<String> fruitNames = new List<String>{'Apple', 'Banana',
'Orange', 'Grapes'};

// Create a list to store Account records
List<Account> fruitAccountsList = new List<Account>();

// Populate the list with Account records
for (String fruit : fruitNames) {
    Account newFruitAccount = new Account(Name=fruit);
    fruitAccountsList.add(newFruitAccount);
}
```

```
// Upsert the Account records using Database.upsert

Database.upsert(fruitAccountsList, false);

// Upsert the Account records
List<Account> upsertedAccounts = [SELECT Id, Name FROM Account WHERE Name
IN :fruitNames];

// Iterate over the upserted records to verify
    for (Account fruitAccount : fruitAccountsList) {
        System.debug('Upserted Fruit Account: ' + fruitAccount);
    }
```

Salesforce will automatically use the Id field to match records. Since we're creating new Account records without specifying Ids, the upsert operation will effectively perform an insert for all records. If any of the records had existing Ids that matched records in the database, those records would be updated instead of inserted.

Update: Used to modify existing records in the database.

```
// Example List of Strings
List<String> fruitNames = new List<String>{'Apple', 'Banana', 'Orange',
'Grapes'};

// Create a list to store Account records
List<Account> fruitAccountsList = [SELECT Id, Name FROM Account
WHERE Name IN :fruitNames];

// Update all account names in the database
for (Account account : fruitAccountsList) {
    account.Name = 'Updated' + account.Name;
    // Prepend 'Updated ' to each name
}

if (!fruitAccountsList.isEmpty()) {
    update fruitAccountsList;

    // Iterate over the updated records to verify
    for (Account updatedFruitAccount : fruitAccountsList) {
        System.debug('Updated Fruit Account: ' + updatedFruitAccount.Name);
    }
```

```
} else {
    System.debug('No matching accounts found to update.');
}
```

In this code, each Account name is updated by prepending 'Updated' to its existing name. These modified names are then used to update the existing Account records in the database. The debug statement will show the updated names of the Account records in the debug logs. If no matching accounts are found, a debug message will indicate this.

Delete: Used to remove records from the database.

```
// Example List of Strings
List<String> fruitAccountsList = new List<String>{'Updated Apple'};

// Query the Account records with the updated alternative names
List<Account> accountsToDelete = [SELECT Id FROM Account WHERE
Name IN :fruitAccountsList];

// Delete the records from the database
delete accountsToDelete;

// Show that the records are deleted
String deletedAccountIds = ' ';
for (Account deletedAccount : accountsToDelete) {
    deletedAccountIds += deletedAccount.Id + ', ';
}
System.debug('Deleted Fruit Account IDs: ' + deletedAccountIds);
```

This code queries the Account records with the updated names and then uses the delete DML operation to delete those records. The debug statement shows the deleted records in the debug logs.

Undelete: Used to restore records that have been previously deleted from the database. This operation is specifically used to recover records that were soft-deleted and placed in the recycle bin rather than permanently removed.

When records are deleted in Salesforce, they are initially moved to the recycle bin where they can be restored or permanently deleted. The undelete operation allows you to retrieve records from there and bring them back into the active database. Here's an example of how *undelete* can be used in Salesforce Apex:

```
// Example List of Strings
List<String> fruitAccountsList =
new List<String>{'Updated Apple'};

// Query the deleted records from the Recycle Bin
List<Account> deletedAccounts = [SELECT Id FROM Account WHERE
Name IN : fruitAccountsList ALL ROWS];

// Undelete the records
Database.undelete(deletedAccounts);

// Query the undeleted records to get their details
List<Account> undeletedAccounts = [SELECT Id, Name FROM Account WHERE Id
IN :deletedAccounts];

// Debug the undeleted accounts
for (Account acc : undeletedAccounts) {
    System.debug('Undeleted Account: ' + acc.Name);
}
```

This code queries the deleted Account records with the updated alternative names from the Salesforce Recycle Bin using the ALL ROWS clause and then uses the Database. undelete method to undelete them. The debug statement shows the undeleted records in the debug logs.

Merge: Is only available for certain standard objects in Salesforce, such as Account, Contact, Lead, and Case, and you can merge up to three records at a time.

```
Account masterAccount = new Account(Name = 'MyName');
insert masterAccount;
Account duplicateAccount = new Account(Name = 'MyName');
insert duplicateAccount;

Database.merge(masterAccount, duplicateAccount);
// Perform the merge operation

// Query the master account to get its updated state
masterAccount = [SELECT Id, Name, (SELECT Id FROM Contacts) FROM Account
WHERE Id = :masterAccount.Id];
```

```
// Verify the result of the merge operation
System.debug('Merged Account Name: ' + masterAccount.Name);
```

It creates an Account record named "MyName" and inserts it into the database. This account will serve as the master account during the merge operation. It creates another Account record with the same name ("MyName") and inserts it into the database. This account is a duplicate that will be merged into the master account.

These DML operations are crucial for interacting with the Salesforce database and performing data-related tasks in your Apex code. It's important to note that DML operations can affect a single record or multiple records using collections like lists or maps, and they ensure proper data integrity and security within the Salesforce platform. Additionally, DML operations might trigger various database events, such triggers and flows, which can execute additional logic based on the data changes.

The governor limit in Salesforce is 150 statements in a transaction, and this limit applies to the total number of DML statements executed in a transaction, regardless of the type of operation or the number of records affected by each statement. For example, if you perform 100 insert statements and 50 update statements, you would have reached the limit of 150 DML statements.

The limit for the number of records that can be processed by Apex DML operations in a single transaction is 10,000. This means to perform insert, update, or delete operations not more than 10,000 records within a single transaction.

You can use Limits.getDMLRows() method to implement logic that checks the number of records affected by DML operations and displays a warning message to the user if the limit is approaching. This can help users avoid hitting the governor limits and take necessary actions to optimize their code.

Here's an example of how you can use Limits.getDMLRows() method to check the number of records affected by DML operations:

```
List<Account> accountsToInsert = new List<Account>();

// Adding sample Account records to the list
accountsToInsert.add(new Account(Name='Account1'));
accountsToInsert.add(new Account(Name='Account2'));
accountsToInsert.add(new Account(Name='Account3'));

// Perform DML operation (insert)
insert accountsToInsert;
```

```
// Check the number of records affected by DML operation
Integer dmlRows = Limits.getDMLRows();
System.debug('Number of records affected by DML operation: ' + dmlRows);
```

In the above example, the insert statement inserts the accountsToInsert list, and then Limits.getDMLRows() method is used to retrieve the number of records affected by the insert operation. If the number 6 or more is being returned by Limits.getDMLRows() after inserting the three sample records, it's because Salesforce counts the records for certain DML operations. For example, when you insert a record that has a master-detail relationship, Salesforce might count not only the parent record you explicitly inserted but also any child records created due to the relationship. In the case of Account records, if you have any child records related through master-detail relationships, they might be counted as well. Make sure that there are no triggers, processes, or other automation that create additional records during the insert operation.

By using Limits.getDMLRows() method, you can have better control over the usage of DML governor limits and optimize your code accordingly.

It's important to note that Limits.getDMLRows() method only returns the number of records affected by DML operations in the current transaction.

Avoiding DML operations inside loops is a best practice in Salesforce Apex to ensure efficient and optimized code execution. Performing DML operations, such as inserts, updates, or deletes, within a loop can lead to performance issues, governor limits breaches, and slow execution times. Instead, you should accumulate the necessary data and perform the DML operation outside the loop. Here's an example to illustrate this best practice:

```
// Define a set to store unique AccountIds
Set<Id> uniqueAccountIds = new Set<Id>();

// Define a list to accumulate data for DML operation
List<Account> accountsToUpdate = new List<Account>();

// Assume you have a loop to retrieve and process data
for (Contact contact : [SELECT Id, AccountId FROM Contact WHERE
AccountId != null LIMIT 10]) {
    // Check if the AccountId is unique before adding to the list
    if (!uniqueAccountIds.contains(contact.AccountId)) {
```

```
    // Perform some processing on the data
    Account acc = new Account(Id = contact.AccountId, Name = 'Updated Name');

    // Add the modified record to the list instead of performing
    // DML inside the loop
    accountsToUpdate.add(acc);

    // Add the AccountId to the set to track uniqueness
    uniqueAccountIds.add(contact.AccountId);
    }
}

// Perform the DML operation outside the loop
update accountsToUpdate;

// Debug statement to verify
System.debug('Updated Accounts: ' + accountsToUpdate);
```

In this example, we use a loop to retrieve Contacts and process them. Instead of updating the Account records within the loop, we accumulate them in a list (accountsToUpdate). After the loop, we perform a single update DML operation on the list outside the loop, which is a more efficient and governor limits-friendly approach. The System.debug statement is used to verify the updated accounts in the debug logs.

5.2 Classes, Interfaces, and Methods

A class is a fundamental component that defines an object's functionality and characteristics. The basic structure of an Apex class consists of class variables also known as properties, and methods defined within the class.

It serves as a template or blueprint from which objects are created and defines the behavior and properties. Properties are variables defined within a class that store data. An object is an instance of a class. Each instance of the class has its own set of values for these variables. To create an object of a class in Apex, you use the "new" keyword followed by the name of the class.

Methods within the class define actions that objects can perform. The method signature consists of several components such as name, return type, and parameter list that define the method and its behavior. In Apex, method signatures must be unique within the same class. This means that you cannot have two methods in the same class with the same name and the same parameter list.

Overloading is allowed in Apex, which means you can have multiple methods with the same name but with different parameter lists within the same class. The compiler differentiates between these methods based on the number or types of parameters. Here's an example of method overloading:

```
public class MyClass {
    public Integer addNumbers(Integer a, Integer b) {
        return a + b;
    }

    public Double addNumbers(Double a, Double b) {
        return a + b;
    }
}
```

In this example, there are two addNumbers methods in the same class. One takes two Integer parameters, and the other takes two Double parameters. They have different method signatures because of the difference in parameter types.

A class can have an optional constructor that is used for initializing objects. When an object is created, the constructor is called to set the initial values of the object's variables.

In the provided code example here, the *MyFruit* class has two class variables, *fruit* and *count*. The class also has an optional constructor. The method *displayInfo* is a *void* method which doesn't return any value. The purpose of the displayInfo method is to output the values of the *fruit* and *count* variables to the debug log.

When an object of the *MyFruit* class is created using the "new" keyword, the *displayInfo* method can be called to display the values of the *fruit* and *count* variables.

```
public class MyFruit {
    // Class variables (also known as member variables or properties)
    String fruit;
    Integer count;

    // Constructor with concrete values
    MyFruit() {
        fruit = 'orange';
        count = 1;
    }
```

```apex
    // Methods (functions defined within the class)
    public void displayInfo() {
        System.debug(fruit);
        System.debug(count);
    }
}
// Creating an object of MyFruit and calling the constructor
MyFruit objectFruit =new myFruit();
objectFruit.displayInfo();
```

Here's another example that demonstrates the usage of constructors in Apex:

```apex
public class Fruit {
    public String name;
    public Integer quantity;

    // Default constructor
    public Fruit() {
        name = 'Unknown';
        quantity = 0;
    }

    // Parameterized constructor
    public Fruit(String name, Integer quantity) {
        this.name = name;
        this.quantity = quantity;
    }

    // Method to display fruit information
    public void displayInfo() {
        System.debug('Fruit Information:');
        System.debug('Name: ' + name);
        System.debug('Quantity: ' + quantity);
    }

    // Method to check if the fruit is in abundance (example)
    public Boolean isInAbundance() {
        // Assuming fruits with a quantity greater than 100 are
        // considered in abundance
```

```
        return quantity > 100;
    }
}
```

//You can use this Fruit class by creating instances of it, setting properties, and calling its methods.

```
Fruit myFruit = new Fruit('Apple', 150);
myFruit.displayInfo();
System.debug('Is it in abundance? ' + myFruit.isInAbundance());
```

This example demonstrates how to use the new Fruit class with the adjusted properties and methods.

Overall, the basic process of creating an object of a class with an optional constructor involves calling the constructor to initialize the object's variables and then calling any methods defined within the class on the object. Here are some key points about constructors in Apex:

- A constructor has the same name as the class it belongs to.

- The access specifier for a constructor is typically public.

- Constructors are invoked automatically when an object is created using the new keyword.

- Constructors can be used to set default or required values for an object when it is first created.

- If a class does not have a user-defined constructor, a default, no-argument, public constructor is provided by the compiler.

- Constructors can be overloaded, meaning a class can have multiple constructors with different parameter lists.

- Constructors can perform initialization tasks, such as assigning values to instance variables or calling other methods.

The next important aspect of classes is understanding access modifiers. In Apex, access modifiers determine the visibility and accessibility of classes, methods, and variables in your code. Access modifiers can be also used to control the visibility and accessibility of variables and methods in Apex only within the class where they are declared. There are three main access modifiers for classes in Apex: global, public, and private.

Global keyword is used in Apex to define a class or method as accessible outside of the package. A Global class can be accessed by other classes in different namespaces or by external systems, such as web services. The Global class is commonly used in the following scenarios:

- *Creating Web Services*: Apex classes with the Global access modifier can be exposed as web services, allowing external systems to invoke their methods and exchange data with Salesforce.

- *Integration with External Systems*: By defining a Global class, you can establish a connection between Salesforce and external systems, enabling the exchange of data and functionality.

- *Managed Packages*: If you are developing a managed package, you can use Global classes to expose specific methods or functionality to other organizations that install your package.

Here's a simple example:

Step 1: Open Developer Console ➤ File ➤ New ➤ Apex class ➤ insert the code

```
global class MyManagedPackageClass {
    // A method that is exposed for use by organizations installing the
    managed package
    global static String processData(String input) {
        // Some logic to process the input data
        return 'Processed data: ' + input;
    }

    // Another method that is exposed
    global static Integer calculateSum(Integer a, Integer b) {
        // Some logic to calculate the sum
        return a + b;
    }
}
```

Step 2: Save the new class

Step 3: Open the anonymous window

Step 4: Execute the global class

```
// Call global methods from the managed package in the anonymous window

String result = MyManagedPackageClass.processData('Input data');
Integer sum = MyManagedPackageClass.calculateSum(3, 5);

System.debug('Result: ' + result);
System.debug('Sum: ' + sum);
```

After packaging and distributing your managed package, other organizations can use these global methods in their Apex code. This allows you to provide specific functionality to organizations that have installed your managed package while encapsulating other parts of your code to maintain a level of control and encapsulation.

Public class is a class that can be accessed by other classes and triggers within the same Salesforce org. It is the default access modifier for classes in Apex, meaning that if no access modifier is specified, the class is automatically considered public. Common use cases for public classes are

- *Controller Classes*: Public classes are often used as controller classes in the Model-View-Controller (MVC) architecture in Salesforce. These classes handle the logic and data manipulation for Visualforce pages or Lightning web components.

- *Batch Apex*: Public classes are used to define batch Apex jobs, which allow for the processing of large datasets in smaller chunks. Batch Apex classes implement the Database.Batchable interface and provide methods for processing records in batches.

- *REST Callouts*: Public classes can be used to make HTTP callouts to external services or APIs. These classes implement the HttpCalloutMock interface and provide methods for sending and receiving data over HTTP.

- *Test Classes*: Public classes are also used to write test classes for unit testing Apex code. Test classes are responsible for verifying the behavior and functionality of Apex classes and methods.

In this example, the public class serves as a simple controller:

```
public class SimpleControllerExample {

    public String greeting { get; set; }

    public SimpleControllerExample() {
        greeting = 'Hello, Salesforce!';
    }

    public void updateGreeting(String newGreeting) {
        greeting = newGreeting;
    }
}

// Instantiate the controller and test its methods
SimpleControllerExample myController = new SimpleControllerExample();

// Print the initial greeting
System.debug('Initial Greeting: ' + myController.greeting);

// Update the greeting
myController.updateGreeting('New Greeting');

// Print the updated greeting
System.debug('Updated Greeting: ' + myController.greeting);
```

This code demonstrates the basic concepts of a controller class, even though it's not connected to a user interface. It's a simple way to showcase the functionality of a class in the anonymous window.

Private class is a class that can only be accessed within the same Apex class or trigger in which it is defined. It cannot be accessed outside of the class or trigger, including within other classes or triggers in the same Salesforce organization. Private classes are primarily used for encapsulating functionality that is specific to a particular class or trigger, and are not intended to be used externally. Access modifiers can be also used to control the visibility and accessibility of variables and methods in Apex only within the class where they are declared. Here is an example for private access modifier within the classPrivate classes that are commonly used in Apex for the following purposes:

- *Helper Classes*: Private classes can be used as helper classes within a larger class or trigger to encapsulate complex or reusable logic that is specific to that class or trigger. This helps in organizing and modularizing the code, making it easier to read and maintain.

- *Inner Classes*: Private classes can be defined as inner classes within another class. Inner classes have access to the variables and methods of the outer class, allowing for tighter integration and sharing of data.

- *Data Structures*: Private classes can be used to define custom data structures that are used internally within a class or trigger. These data structures can hold related data and provide methods for manipulating and accessing that data.

Here's a simple example:

```
Step 1: Create the private class
public class MyOuterClass {
    private class MyPrivateClass {
        public void myMethod() {
            System.debug('Hello PrivateClass');
        }
    }

    private Integer count = 2;

    public void callPrivateMethod() {
        MyPrivateClass obj = new MyPrivateClass();
        obj.myMethod();
        displayInfo();
    }

    public void displayInfo() {
        System.debug(count);
    }

    public Integer getCount() {
        return count;
    }
}
```

Step 2: Save the class

Step 3: Open the anonymous window

Step 4: Test the public class
```
MyOuterClass outerInstance = new MyOuterClass();
outerInstance.callPrivateMethod();
Integer countValue = outerInstance.getCount();
System.debug('Count from getCount method: ' + countValue);
```

In this code block MyOuterClass now includes both the private inner class *MyPrivateClass* and the private variable *count. The callPrivateMethod* method demonstrates calling the private method *myMethod* from *MyPrivateClass,* and it also calls the *displayInfo method t*o show the value of the private variable *count.* Finally, it calls the *getCount* method to demonstrate accessing the private variable directly.

Extend keyword in Apex is used to define a class that extends another class. When a class extends another class, it inherits all the properties and methods from the parent class, allowing you to reuse code and add additional functionality specific to the child class.

Step 1: Create the ParentClass
```
public virtual class ParentClass {
    public void displayMessage() {
        System.debug('Hello from ParentClass');
    }
}
```

Step 2: Save the ParentClass
Step 3: Create the ChildClass
```
public class ChildClass extends ParentClass {
    public void displayChildMessage() {
        System.debug('Hello from ChildClass');
    }
}
```

Step 4: Save the ChildClass
Step 5: Open the anonymous window

Step 6: Test the ParentClass and ChildClass
```
// Example usage in the Anonymous Apex window
ChildClass childInstance = new ChildClass();
childInstance.displayMessage();
// This will call the method from ParentClass
childInstance.displayChildMessage();
// This will call the method from ChildClass
```

In this example, *ChildClass* extends *ParentClass*. This means that *ChildClass* inherits the *displayMessage* method from *ParentClass*. Additionally, *ChildClass* has its own method *displayChildMessage*. When you create an instance of *ChildClass* and call its methods, it will execute both the inherited method from the parent class and its own method.

Apex also supports inner classes, which are classes defined within another class. Inner classes have access to the properties and methods of the outer class. You can create an instance of an inner class within the outer class or outside the outer class, similar to any other class.

In the below example, the OuterClass class contains an inner class called InnerClass.

Step 1: Create the class
```
public class OuterClass {
    public class InnerClass {
        public void displayMessage() {
            System.debug('Hello from InnerClass');
        }
    }
}
```
Step 2: Save the class

Step 3: Open the anonymous window

Step 4: Test the outer class
```
// Example usage in the Anonymous Apex window
OuterClass outerInstance = new OuterClass();
OuterClass.InnerClass innerInstance = new OuterClass.InnerClass();

innerInstance.displayMessage();
```

An interface in Apex specifies a set of methods that implementing classes must provide. Interfaces enable a form of multiple inheritance, allowing a class to implement multiple interfaces. It is similar to a class, but it does not have any of its methods implemented. Instead, each method's body is empty, and only the method signatures are present. It could be defined using the interface keyword, followed by the interface name and declare method signatures without providing the implementation.

Let's consider a scenario where you are developing a custom Salesforce application for a university. In this application, you need to create a class that represents a student. The Student class should implement two interfaces: Enrollable and ScholarshipEligible.

First, let's define the two interfaces:

```
// Interface Definitions
public interface Enrollable {
    void enroll();
}

public interface ScholarshipEligible {
    Boolean isEligibleForScholarship();
}

// Student Class Implementing Interfaces
public class Student implements Enrollable, ScholarshipEligible {
    private String name;
    private Boolean enrolled;
    private Boolean hasGoodGrades;

    public Student(String name, Boolean hasGoodGrades) {
        this.name = name;
        this.hasGoodGrades = hasGoodGrades;
        this.enrolled = false;
// Newly created student is not enrolled by default
    }

    public void enroll() {
        enrolled = true;
        System.debug(name + ' has been enrolled.');
    }
```

```
    public Boolean isEligibleForScholarship() {
        return hasGoodGrades;
    }
}
// Usage Example by creating new instances
Student student1 = new Student('John Doe', true);
student1.enroll(); // Output: John Doe has been enrolled.
Boolean isEligible1 = student1.isEligibleForScholarship();
System.debug('Is eligible for scholarship: ' + isEligible1);
// Output: Is eligible for scholarship: true

Student student2 = new Student('Jane Smith', false);
student2.enroll(); // Output: Jane Smith has been enrolled.
Boolean isEligible2 = student2.isEligibleForScholarship();
System.debug('Is eligible for scholarship: ' + isEligible2);
// Output: Is eligible for scholarship: false
```

In this code block, the interface definitions, the Student class, and the usage example are combined. You can execute this code as an anonymous Apex block in the Developer Console. This code will create Student objects, enroll them, and check their scholarship eligibility. The debug logs will display the output messages.

By implementing multiple interfaces, you can define different sets of behaviors for your classes and achieve more flexible and modular code.

Interface methods are implicitly public and cannot be modified. Implementing classes must adhere to this visibility. Both classes and interfaces are fundamental to building well-organized, modular, and maintainable applications on the Salesforce platform.

Apex includes a variety of method-related keywords such as static, virtual, global, abstract, and instance which empower developers to create efficient, modular, and extensible code:

Static Methods

- A static method belongs to the class itself, not to instances of the class.

- It can be called using the class name, without creating an instance of the class.

- Static methods cannot access instance variables, but they can access other static variables or other static methods.

Let's say you have a class called StringUtil that contains a static method called capitalizeFirstLetter. This method takes a string as input and returns the string with the first letter capitalized. Here's how the code would look:

```
Step 1: Create the class
public class StringUtil {
    public static String capitalizeFirstLetter(String input) {
        if (String.isBlank(input)) {
            return input;
        }

        return input.substring(0, 1).toUpperCase() + input.substring(1);
    }
}
Step 2: Save the class
Step 3: Open the anonymous window
Step 4: Test the public class
// Example usage in the Anonymous Apex window
String inputString = 'hello';
String capitalizedString = StringUtil.capitalizeFirstLetter(inputString);
System.debug('Original String: ' + inputString);
System.debug('Capitalized String: ' + capitalizedString);
```

To use this static method, you can call it directly on the class name, without creating an instance of the StringUtil class. The provided Apex code above capitalizes the first letter of a given string using a static method in the StringUtil class.

This is just one example of how you can use Apex static methods. They are flexible and can be used in various scenarios to perform specific tasks without the need to create an instance of the class.

Virtual Methods

In Apex, a virtual method is a method declared in a base class that can be overridden in its subclasses. This allows you to provide different implementations of the method in different subclasses. This concept is useful when you want to define a common behavior in a base class, but allow its subclasses to customize or extend that behavior.

In the given example, we start with a base class named Item, which defines a virtual method called calculateProperty(). The intention is to create specialized subclasses, such as Car and Bicycle, each offering its own unique implementation of the calculateProperty() method.

```
public class Item {
    public virtual void calculateProperty() {
        System.debug('Calculating some property of the item');
    }
}

public class Car extends Item {
    private Decimal fuelEfficiency;

    public Car(Decimal fuelEfficiency) {
        this.fuelEfficiency = fuelEfficiency;
    }

    public override void calculateProperty() {
        Decimal distance = 100;
    // Assume a constant distance for simplicity
        Decimal fuelConsumed = distance / fuelEfficiency;
        System.debug('Calculating fuel consumption of the car: ' +
            fuelConsumed);
    }
}

public class Bicycle extends Item {
    private Decimal distanceTraveled;

    public Bicycle(Decimal distanceTraveled) {
        this.distanceTraveled = distanceTraveled;
    }

    public override void calculateProperty() {
        System.debug('Calculating distance traveled by the bicycle: ' +
            distanceTraveled);
    }
}
```

```
// Usage
Item genericItem = new Item();
genericItem.calculateProperty();
// Output: Calculating some property of the item

Item car = new Car(10);  // Car with fuel efficiency 10
car.calculateProperty();
// Output: Calculating fuel consumption of the car: 10.0

Item bicycle = new Bicycle(50);  // Bicycle with 50 km distance traveled
bicycle.calculateProperty();
// Output: Calculating distance traveled by the bicycle: 50.0
```

When we instantiate an object from the Item class and invoke the calculateProperty() method, the output is "Calculating some property of the item," reflecting the generic nature of the base class.

On the other hand, creating instances of the Car and Bicycle classes and calling their respective calculateProperty() methods yields distinctive outputs. For a Car instance with a fuel efficiency of 10, invoking calculateProperty() results in "Calculating fuel consumption of the car: 10.0." Similarly, for a Bicycle instance that has traveled 50 km, invoking calculateProperty() produces "Calculating distance traveled by the bicycle: 50.0."

This example illustrates how the use of a virtual method allows for the encapsulation of diverse calculations, showcasing the flexibility of the object-oriented paradigm in tailoring behavior based on specific subclasses.

Global Methods

A global method has the highest level of visibility and can be accessed from other classes, triggers, and even external systems, like managed packages or web services. They are often used to define entry points for integration with external systems.

```
Step 1: Create the class and save
global class MyGlobalClass {
    global Integer myGlobalMethod() {
        // Your code here
        return 5; // Example return statement
    }
}
```

In this example, the MyGlobalClass has a global method myGlobalMethod that returns an integer value.

Step 2: Create another class and save

```
public class MyCallingClass {
    public static void callGlobalMethod() {
        MyGlobalClass myGlobalInstance = new MyGlobalClass();
        Integer result = myGlobalInstance.myGlobalMethod();
        System.debug('Result: ' + result); // Example debug statement
    }
}
```

In this example, the MyCallingClass has a public static method callGlobalMethod. This method creates an instance of MyGlobalClass and calls the myGlobalMethod on it. The result of the myGlobalMethod is stored in the result variable and debugged.

Step 3: Open the anonymous window

Step 4: Test the global class

```
MyCallingClass.callGlobalMethod();
```

This will execute the myGlobalMethod from the MyGlobalClass and print the result in the debug log.

Remember that global methods have some limitations and considerations. They can only be used in certain contexts, such as in managed packages or with certain APIs. Additionally, global methods can expose sensitive data if not properly secured, so make sure to implement any necessary access controls and validations within the method itself.

Abstract Methods

- An abstract method is a method declared in a class but does not have an implementation in that class.

- Subclasses must provide implementations for all abstract methods.

- An abstract class can also contain non-abstract methods.

In the example below, let's consider an abstract class named Item that represents a generic item, and we want to define a method called calculateProperty() to calculate some property of the item. However, since the calculation of this property may vary for different types of items, we declare the calculateProperty() method as abstract in the abstract class Item. This indicates that any concrete subclass of Item must provide its own implementation of the calculateProperty() method.

```
// Abstract class
public abstract class Item {
    // Abstract method to calculate some property
    public abstract Decimal calculateProperty();

    // Concrete method
    public void printDetails() {
        System.debug('This is an item.');
    }
}

// Subclass representing a car item
public class CarItem extends Item {
    private Decimal fuelEfficiency;

    // Constructor
    public CarItem(Decimal fuelEfficiency) {
        this.fuelEfficiency = fuelEfficiency;
    }

    // Implementing the abstract method to calculate fuel consumption
    public override Decimal calculateProperty() {
        Decimal distance = 100;
    // Assume a constant distance for simplicity
        Decimal fuelConsumed = distance / fuelEfficiency;
        System.debug('Calculating fuel consumption of the car:' +
            fuelConsumed);
        return fuelConsumed;
    }
}
```

```
// Subclass representing a bicycle item
public class BicycleItem extends Item {
    private Decimal distanceTraveled;

    // Constructor
    public BicycleItem(Decimal distanceTraveled) {
        this.distanceTraveled = distanceTraveled;
    }

    // Implementing the abstract method to calculate distance traveled
    public override Decimal calculateProperty() {
        System.debug('Calculating distance traveled by the bicycle: ' +
        distanceTraveled);
        return distanceTraveled;
    }
}

public class Main {
    public void executeMain() {
        // Create an instance of the CarItem class
        CarItem carItem = new CarItem(10);

        // Call the calculateProperty method
        Decimal fuelConsumed = carItem.calculateProperty();
        System.debug('Fuel consumed by the car: ' + fuelConsumed);

        // Call the printDetails method inherited from the Item class

        carItem.printDetails();

        // Create an instance of the BicycleItem class
        BicycleItem bicycleItem = new BicycleItem(50);

        // Call the calculateProperty method
        Decimal distanceTraveled = bicycleItem.calculateProperty();
        System.debug('Distance traveled by the bicycle: ' +
        distanceTraveled);
```

```
    // Call the printDetails method inherited from the Item class

    bicycleItem.printDetails();
  }
}

// Instantiate the Main class and execute the main method
Main mainInstance = new Main();
mainInstance.executeMain();
```

The abstract class Item contains the abstract method calculateProperty() and a concrete method printDetails(). The calculateProperty() method is declared as abstract, meaning it has no implementation in the abstract class and must be implemented in any subclass that extends Item. The printDetails() method, on the other hand, is a concrete method with an implementation in the abstract class. Subclasses can inherit and use this method without providing their own implementation.

We then have concrete subclasses, such as CarItem and BicycleItem, that extend the Item class. Each of these subclasses provides its own specific implementation of the abstract calculateProperty() method.

For instance, the CarItem class represents an item that is a car. It has a private instance variable fuelEfficiency and a constructor to initialize it. The calculateProperty() method is implemented in CarItem by calculating the fuel consumption of the car based on a constant distance.

Similarly, the BicycleItem class represents an item that is a bicycle. It has a private instance variable distanceTraveled and a constructor to initialize it. The calculateProperty() method is implemented in BicycleItem by calculating the distance traveled by the bicycle.

In the Main class, we create instances of both CarItem and BicycleItem. For the CarItem, we calculate and print the fuel consumed by the car, and for the BicycleItem, we calculate and print the distance traveled by the bicycle. This example demonstrates how an abstract method can be used to define a common method signature in the abstract class and ensure that each concrete subclass provides its own specific implementation, allowing for polymorphic behavior based on the type of item.

Override Method

Apex also supports overriding from method, which allows a child class to provide a different implementation for a method that is already implemented in its parent class. When a child class overrides a method, it provides its own implementation of the method, which is used instead of the implementation in the parent class when the method is called on an instance of the child class. But static methods are associated with the class itself and not with instances of the class. Therefore, they cannot be overridden by child classes.

Let's say we have a parent class called Vehicle with a method called startEngine(). The startEngine() method in the Vehicle class has a default implementation that simply outputs "Engine started."

Step 1: Create the class vehicle and save

```
public virtual class Vehicle {
    public virtual void startEngine() {
        System.debug('Engine started.');
    }
}
```
Step 2: Create the class car and save

```
public class Car extends Vehicle {
        public override void startEngine() {
        System.debug('Car engine started.');
        System.debug('Step on the gas pedal.');
    }
}
```
Step 3: Open the anonymous window

Step 4: Create the new instance of the car

```
        Car car = new Car();
        car.startEngine();
```

The Vehicle class serves as the parent class and contains a method called startEngine(). This method has a default implementation that outputs "Engine started."

The Car class is a child class that extends the Vehicle class. It overrides the startEngine() method from the parent class to provide a different implementation specific to a car. In this case, it outputs "Car engine started." and "Step on the gas pedal."

This demonstrates how the override keyword in Apex allows us to override methods from parent classes and provide custom implementations in child classes.

5.3 Schema Classes and Methods

The Schema class in Apex is a powerful class that allows developers to retrieve metadata information about objects, fields, and record types in Salesforce. It is part of the System namespace and provides methods to dynamically access and manipulate metadata at runtime.

Here are some common use cases for the Schema class:

- *Object and Field Metadata*: You can use the "Schema" class to retrieve information about objects and their fields, such as the object label, API name, data type, picklist values, field accessibility, and more. This can be useful when you need to perform dynamic logic based on the metadata of an object or its fields.

- *Record Type Information*: The "Schema" class allows you to access record type information for objects. You can retrieve details about record types, such as their label, developer name, ID, and whether they are active or not. This information can be used to customize behavior or display different layouts based on the record type.

- *Dynamic Queries and DML Operations*: The "Schema" class enables you to dynamically construct queries and DML operations based on the metadata of objects and fields. For example, you can dynamically build a query to retrieve all fields of an object or dynamically create a record based on the fields available on an object.

- *Integration and Callouts*: When integrating with external systems or making callouts, the "Schema" class can be used to generate the appropriate XML or JSON request payloads based on the metadata of objects and fields. This ensures that the data sent to external systems is in the correct format.

- *Validation and Error Handling*: By using the "Schema" class, you can perform validation checks on user input or data before performing operations. You can verify field lengths, data types, picklist values, and more to ensure data integrity and provide meaningful error messages to users.

Here's an example of how you can use the "Schema" classes in Apex to dynamically retrieve information about objects and record types in Salesforce:

```
// Get the object describe for the Account object
Schema.DescribeSObjectResult accountDescribe =
Account.sObjectType.getDescribe();

// Get the object describe for the Contact object
Schema.DescribeSObjectResult contactDescribe =
Contact.sObjectType.getDescribe();

// Get the object describe for the Opportunity object
Schema.DescribeSObjectResult opportunityDescribe =
Opportunity.sObjectType.getDescribe();

// Retrieve the object label, API name, and record type
// information for each object
String accountLabel = accountDescribe.getLabel();
String accountApiName = accountDescribe.getName();
Map<String, Schema.RecordTypeInfo> accountRecordTypes =
accountDescribe.getRecordTypeInfosByName();

String contactLabel = contactDescribe.getLabel();
String contactApiName = contactDescribe.getName();
Map<String, Schema.RecordTypeInfo> contactRecordTypes =
contactDescribe.getRecordTypeInfosByName();

String opportunityLabel = opportunityDescribe.getLabel();
String opportunityApiName = opportunityDescribe.getName();
Map<String, Schema.RecordTypeInfo> opportunityRecordTypes =
opportunityDescribe.getRecordTypeInfosByName();

// Print the retrieved information
System.debug('Account Object - Label:' + accountLabel +
'API Name:' + accountApiName);
System.debug('Account Record Types:' + accountRecordTypes.keySet());

System.debug('Contact Object - Label:' + contactLabel +
'API Name:' + contactApiName);
```

```
System.debug('Contact Record Types:' + contactRecordTypes.keySet());

System.debug('Opportunity Object - Label:' + opportunityLabel +
'API Name:' + opportunityApiName);
System.debug('Opportunity Record Types:' +
opportunityRecordTypes.keySet());
```

In this example, we use the getDescribe() method on the sObject type to retrieve the DescribeSObjectResult object for each object (Account, Contact, and Opportunity). From the DescribeSObjectResult object, we can access various properties such as the object label, API name, and record type information using the getLabel(), getName(), and getRecordTypeInfosByName() methods, respectively.

The getRecordTypeInfosByName() method returns a map of record type names to RecordTypeInfo objects, which contain information about each record type, such as its label, API name, and whether it is available or not.

Please note that the Schema class is subject to Salesforce platform limits and permissions. You should ensure that your code has appropriate access and permissions to retrieve and manipulate metadata information.

5.4 Database.Batchable Interface

Batchable Apex in Salesforce is an approach to process large volumes of data in smaller, manageable chunks or batches. It enables you to break down the data processing into multiple iterations, each handling a subset of the total data. This approach helps you stay within Salesforce's governor limits and ensures efficient processing of large datasets.

To use it you need to write an Apex class that implements the Database.Batchable interface and then invoke the class programmatically. The Database.Batchable interface contains three methods that developers need to implement: start(), execute(), and finish(). The start() method is called at the beginning of the batch job and returns a Database.QueryLocator object that identifies the scope of the data to be processed. The execute() method processes each batch of records returned by the start() method, and the finish() method is called after all batches are processed.

The maximum batch size is 200 now and can be specified using `Database.executeBatch()` method.

Here's a simple example of the Batch Apex class structure in Salesforce. This class is designed to process leads conversion.

Step 1: Create the class LeadConversionBatch and save

```
global class LeadConversionBatch implements Database.Batchable<SObject>
{
    global Database.QueryLocator start(Database.BatchableContext context)
{
        String query = 'SELECT Id, FirstName, LastName, Email, Company ' +
        'FROM Lead WHERE IsConverted = false AND Status = \'Qualified\'';
        return Database.getQueryLocator(query);
}

    global void execute(Database.BatchableContext context, List<Lead>
    leadRecords) {
        List<Database.LeadConvert> leadsToConvert =
        new List<Database.LeadConvert>();

        for (Lead lead : leadRecords) {
            Database.LeadConvert lc = new Database.LeadConvert();
            lc.setLeadId(lead.Id);
            lc.setConvertedStatus('Qualified'); // Use appropriate status
            leadsToConvert.add(lc);
        }

        if (!leadsToConvert.isEmpty()) {
            try {
                List<Database.LeadConvertResult> lcr =
                Database.convertLead(leadsToConvert);
                // Process the results if needed
            } catch (Exception e) {
                // Handle any exceptions
            }
        }
    }
```

```
    global void finish(Database.BatchableContext context) {
        // Any post-processing logic can go here
    }
}
```

Step 2: Open the anonymous window

Step 3: Insure you have already some leads in your org converted

Step 4: Print the Batch Job ID to the debug log in the Developer Console.

```
// Execute the batch job immediately
LeadConversionBatch leadBatch = new LeadConversionBatch();
String jobId = Database.executeBatch(leadBatch);

// Print the job ID for reference
System.debug('Batch Job ID: ' + jobId);
```

- The start method is the starting point of the batch job. It returns a Database.QueryLocator that defines the initial set of records to be processed. In this case, it selects leads that meet specific criteria: those with the IsConverted field set to false and Status set to 'Qualified'.

- The execute method processes a batch of leads retrieved by the start method. This method is called for each batch of records.

  It creates a list of Database.LeadConvert objects for each lead in the batch. For each lead, it sets the lead ID and the converted status to 'Qualified'.

  It then attempts to convert these leads using the Database. convertLead() method. The method includes error handling to catch any exceptions that might occur during the conversion process.

- The finish method is called after all batches have been processed. In this implementation, it's left empty but can include any additional logic that should run after the batch job is complete.

- The purpose of this Batch Apex class is to convert qualified, unconverted leads into contacts, accounts, and potentially opportunities in batches. By processing leads in batches, it can handle large volumes of data more efficiently and comply with Salesforce's governor limits.

- The class doesn't directly create Contact or Account objects. Instead, it uses Salesforce's standard lead conversion process (Database. convertLead()), which automatically creates these records based on the lead information.

Keep in mind that executing batch jobs directly in an anonymous window is typically done for testing purposes. In a production environment, it's more common to schedule batch jobs using the Salesforce UI or in a separate Apex ScheduledApex class.

5.5 NullPointerException

In Apex, a NullPointerException occurs when you attempt to access or manipulate an object that is null. In other words, you are trying to perform an operation on an object reference that doesn't point to any instance of an object. This can lead to runtime errors and unexpected behavior in your Apex code.

To address this issue the Safe Navigation Operator in Apex, denoted by (?.), is a useful feature that allows you to safely access properties and methods of an object that may be null, without throwing a NullPointerException. It is used to perform null checks before accessing object properties or invoking methods, ensuring that the code doesn't break if the object is null.

The Safe Navigation Operator works by checking if the object is null before accessing its property or invoking a method. If the object is null, the operator returns null instead of throwing a NullPointerException. If the object is not null, the property or method is accessed normally.

Here's a simple example to illustrate the use of the Safe Navigation Operator:

```
Step 1: Create the class MyClass and save
public class MyClass {
    public String getName() {
        return 'John';
    }
}
```

```
Step 2: Open the anonymous window
// Without Safe Navigation Operator
MyClass myObject = null;
String name = myObject.getName();
```

```
System.debug('Name: ' + name);
// This would throw a NullPointerException

// With Safe Navigation Operator
MyClass myObject = null;
String name = myObject?.getName();
System.debug('Name: ' + name); // This will output: null
```

In the code above, if you uncomment the line without the Safe Navigation Operator and run it with myObject being null, it would throw a NullPointerException. However, by using the Safe Navigation Operator, the code with myObject?.getName() will not throw an exception; instead, it assigns null to the name variable.

This concept is generally related to methods in Apex, but it can also be applied to properties and collections to avoid NullPointerException when accessing or manipulating them.

CHAPTER 6

SOQL and SOSL

6.1 Salesforce Object Query Language (SOQL)

Salesforce Object Query Language (SOQL) is a query language used to retrieve data from Salesforce databases. It is similar to SQL (Structured Query Language) but has some syntax differences and is designed specifically for querying Salesforce objects.

SOQL allows developers to query data from a single object or from multiple related objects in the database. It is commonly used to retrieve specific records or to search for records that meet certain criteria. With SOQL you can specify the fields you want to retrieve, filter the records based on conditions, and sort the results.

The basic structure of a Salesforce Object Query Language (SOQL) query follows a specific format, and here is the typical structure:

Step 1: Open the Salesforce Developer Console.

Step 2: In the Developer Console, click on the "Query Editor" tab.

```
SELECT Id, Name, Owner.Name
FROM Account
WHERE Name LIKE 'MyAccount'
ORDER BY Owner.Name
```

Step 3: In the Query Editor, enter your SOQL query. For your example, you can copy and paste the code above. You can change to another name within your existing accounts.

Step: 4 After entering the query, click the "Execute" button (it looks like a play button) to run the query.

Step 5: The results of your query will be displayed in the Query Editor's Results tab. In this example:

SELECT Id, Name, Owner.Name specifies the fields to be retrieved.

© Konstantin Kapitanov 2024
K. Kapitanov, *Salesforce Developer I Certification*, Certification Study Companion Series,
https://doi.org/10.1007/979-8-8688-0300-0_6

FROM Account specifies the object from which to retrieve data (in this case, the Account object).

WHERE Name = 'MyAccount' is the optional WHERE clause used to filter records.

ORDER BY Owner.Name is the optional ORDER BY clause used to sort the results.

You can build more complex queries by combining these clauses and using features like subqueries for related data and aggregate functions for calculations.

SOQL supports aggregate functions like COUNT, SUM, AVG, MAX, and MIN. These functions can be used to perform calculations on groups of records and retrieve summarized data. For example:

```
SELECT Industry, AVG(AnnualRevenue)
FROM Account
GROUP BY Industry
HAVING AVG(AnnualRevenue) > 1000000
```

Aggregate functions in SOQL are essential for summarizing and analyzing data within Salesforce objects. They allow you to generate reports and metrics to gain insights into your business data, such as calculating totals, averages, and counts within specific criteria or groups.

SOQL queries respect Salesforce's security and access control settings like field-level security and permission sets. Users can only query data they have the necessary permissions to access.

The LIMIT function can be used to restrict the number of records returned by a query. For example:

```
SELECT Name, Industry FROM Account LIMIT 10
```

This query retrieves the names and industries of the first 10 accounts in the Salesforce database. The LIMIT clause limits the result set to 10 records.

However, SOQL queries are subject to governor limits, such as 100 SOQL queries issued synchronous or 200 queries in an asynchronous transaction, or the maximum number of records returned per transaction is 50,000. In the row limit if you have a query with three parent-child relationships for example, it will still count as one query, but the row limit will be reduced to 2,000. This limit applies to the combined result set of all records retrieved, including records from the primary object and any related objects. Each related object contributes to the overall row count, so if you have multiple related objects in your query, the sum of their rows must not exceed the total query row limit.

When you're working with parent and child records, you are typically dealing with related objects in Salesforce. Salesforce uses a relationship model to link records from different objects together. Understanding how to query and navigate these relationships is crucial when you need to access data from both parent and child records. Let's come back to the key concepts related to parent and child records in SOQL. Salesforce objects are related to one another through various types of relationships, such as the following.

- *Lookup Relationship*: This is a simple parent-child relationship where a child record has a reference (lookup) to a parent record. For example, an Opportunity may have a lookup to an Account, making Account the parent object.

- *Master-Detail Relationship*: This is a stricter form of parent-child relationship, where child records (detail) are considered subordinate to the parent record (master). Deleting a master record also deletes its related detail records.

- *Hierarchical Relationship*: This type of relationship is unique to the user object in Salesforce. For example, a user may have a manager as another user.

Navigating through parent-child relationships in SOQL refers to the ability to traverse and query data across related objects in Salesforce using SOQL. Parent-child relationships exist when one object is related to another object, such as a master-detail or lookup relationship. For example, if you have a parent object called "Account" and a child object called "Contact," you can use a SOQL query to retrieve information from both objects. However, the number of child records levels that can be returned in a single SOQL query from one parent object is one. Here's an example:

```
SELECT Id, Name, (SELECT Id, FirstName, LastName FROM Contacts)
FROM Account
```

In this query, we are retrieving the Account's Id and Name fields, as well as the related Contacts' Id, FirstName, and LastName fields. The (SELECT FROM Contacts) part of the query is known as a subquery and allows you to retrieve data from the child object.

The data types that can be returned from any SOQL request include the following:

- *Single sObject*: An SOQL query can return a single sObject record. This is useful when you want to retrieve and work with a specific record or object, typically used with LIMIT 1 in the query.

- *List of sObjects*: An SOQL query can return a list of sObjects. This is useful when you want to retrieve multiple records or objects that meet certain criteria.

- *Integer*: This is typically returned when using aggregate functions like COUNT(). It's useful for getting a count of records that meet certain criteria.

- *AggregateResult*: An SOQL query can return an AggregateResult object by using aggregate functions like COUNT, SUM, MAX, MIN, AVG with a GROUP BY or without. These functions group and summarize data, potentially reducing the number of rows in the result set. For example, if you use GROUP BY on a field, the query may return fewer rows because it groups similar values together.

Dynamic SOQL refers to the ability to construct and execute SOQL queries dynamically at runtime, rather than having the query hardcoded in your Apex code. Dynamic SOQL allows you to construct queries based on runtime conditions or user inputs. You can dynamically adjust various parts of your query, including the fields to select, the object to query, and the conditions in the WHERE clause. This provides flexibility when you need to create queries with variable criteria or when the object and field names are not known until runtime. It can be executed using the Database.query() method.

Here is an example of a simple dynamic Salesforce SOQL query you can test in Anonymous Window:

To to Setup ➤ Developer Console Debug ➤ Open Execute Anonymous Window, put the code block and press on Execute button.

```
String objectName = 'Account';
String fieldName = 'Name';
String fieldValue = 'Myname'; // Replace with the desired account name
```

```
String queryString = 'SELECT Id, ' + fieldName + ' FROM ' +
objectName + ' WHERE ' + fieldName + ' LIKE \'%' + fieldValue + '%\'';
List<sObject> sList = Database.query(queryString);

for (sObject s : sList) {
    System.debug(s);
}
```

But the construction of dynamic SOQL queries, as shown in the preceding example, can potentially introduce security vulnerabilities if the input values such as fieldValue are not properly sanitized or validated. Constructing queries by concatenating strings without proper handling can lead to SQL injection vulnerabilities.

You can use the String.escapeSingleQuotes method to properly escape single quotes in dynamic SOQL queries in Salesforce. Here's how you can modify your example:

```
String objectName = 'Account';
String fieldName = 'Name';
String fieldValue = 'Myname';
// Replace with the desired account name

// Escape single quotes in the fieldValue variable
String queryString = 'SELECT Id, ' + fieldName + ' FROM ' +
objectName + ' WHERE ' + fieldName +
' LIKE \'%' + String.escapeSingleQuotes(fieldValue) + '%\'';

List<sObject> sList = Database.query(queryString);

for (sObject s : sList) {
    System.debug(s);
}
```

In this modification, String.escapeSingleQuotes is applied to the fieldValue variable to ensure that any single quotes within the value are properly escaped. The escaped value is then used in the dynamic SOQL query.

While using String.escapeSingleQuotes adds an extra layer of protection, it's important to note that using bind variables in your static SOQL queries is generally a better practice for preventing injection vulnerabilities. If possible, consider using bind variables in your queries, as Salesforce automatically handles the necessary escaping when using them. Here's how you can modify your example to use bind variables:

```
String objectName = 'Account';
String fieldName = 'Name';
String fieldValue = 'Myname';
// Replace with the desired account name

// Query using a bind variable in a static query
List<Account> accountList =
[SELECT Id, Name FROM Account WHERE Name = :fieldValue];

for (Account acc : accountList) {
    System.debug(acc);
}
```

In this modified example, *:fieldValue* is a bind variable. It is used in the SOQL query, and Salesforce will automatically handle the proper escaping and processing of the variable, reducing the risk of injection attacks.

6.2 Salesforce Object Search Language (SOSL)

Salesforce Object Search Language (SOSL) is a query language specifically designed for searching records in Salesforce. It allows you to search across multiple standard and custom Salesforce objects simultaneously, making it a powerful tool for finding data that meets specific criteria. SOSL queries can be used in various contexts, such as Apex code, Lightning Web Components, and the Salesforce REST API. Here's a basic explanation of how SOSL works with an example:

Let's say you work for a company that uses Salesforce to manage customer data, and you want to find all records that mention the term "acme" in either the Account Name or Contact Name fields. You could use SOSL to perform this search. SOSL uses the FIND keyword to initiate a search and allows you to specify one or more search terms. Here's a simple SOSL query for our example:

```
FIND {acme} IN ALL FIELDS RETURNING Account, Contact
```

When you execute this SOSL query, Salesforce will search for any records that contain the term "acme" in their fields within the specified objects (Account and Contact). The results will include both Accounts and Contacts that match the search criteria.

When a SOSL query returns multiple lists of sObjects, the result is a list of lists of sObjects. Each list contains the search results for a particular sObject type, and the result lists are always returned in the same order as they were specified in the SOSL query. To handle SOSL query results that contain multiple lists of sObjects, users can use nested for loops to iterate over the lists and extract the data they need. Here is an example of how to handle SOSL query results that contain multiple lists of sObjects:

```
List<List<SObject>> searchResults = [FIND 'apple' IN ALL FIELDS RETURNING
Account (Id, Name), Contact (Id, FirstName, LastName)];
for (List<SObject> resultList : searchResults) {
    for (SObject record : resultList) {
        if (record instanceof Account) {
            Account accountRecord = (Account) record;
            System.debug('Account Name: ' + accountRecord.Name);
            // Do something with the account record
        } else if (record instanceof Contact) {
            Contact contactRecord = (Contact) record;
            System.debug('Contact Name: ' + contactRecord.FirstName +
                ' ' + contactRecord.LastName);
            // Do something with the contact record
        }
    }
}
```

In this example:

1. The SOSL query searches for the term "apple" in all fields of both the Account and Contact objects with specifying specific fields to return.

2. The searchResults variable contains the search results as a list of lists of SObjects, just like in the previous example.

3. The code then iterates through the search results:

   The outer loop iterates over each inner list, which corresponds to the results for either the Account or Contact object.

   The inner loop iterates through each SObject (record) within the inner list.

4. Inside the inner loop, it checks whether each record is an instance of the Account or Contact object using the instanceof operator.

5. Depending on the type of the record, it casts the SObject to either an Account or Contact object and then performs a simple action: printing the Account Name or Contact Name using System.debug().

Keep in mind that SOSL is particularly useful for searching across multiple objects and is designed for searching, not for retrieving detailed record information. If you need to retrieve specific fields of records, you may need to perform subsequent queries using SOQL.

6.3 Create Queries with Best Practice

SOQL (Salesforce Object Query Language) and SOSL (Salesforce Object Search Language) are two query languages used in Salesforce to retrieve data from the database. Here are the main differences between SOQL and SOSL:

SOQL (Salesforce Object Query Language)

- Queries start with the "SELECT" keyword.

- It is used to query data from a single object or related objects.

- It can query any type of field in the database.

- It can be used in classes and triggers.

- DML operations can be performed on the query results.

- Returns records as the result of the query.

SOSL (Salesforce Object Search Language)

- Queries start with the "FIND" keyword.

- It is used to search for specific text across multiple objects.

- SOSL can search on various text-based fields.

- It can be used in classes and triggers.

- DML operations cannot be performed on the search results.

- Returns fields as the result of the search.

In summary, SOQL is used for querying data from single or related objects, while SOSL is used for performing text searches across multiple objects. SOQL returns records, while SOSL returns fields. Additionally, SOQL allows for more flexibility in querying different types of fields, whereas SOSL is limited to specific field types.

One common best practice to avoid exceeding governor limits is to avoid using SOQL statements inside loops. It can lead to performance issues and can quickly consume governor limits, such as the maximum number of SOQL queries, or CPU time allowed. This can result in errors like "System.LimitException".

By moving the SOQL query outside of the loop, you avoid the query inside the loop problem and can handle the updates more efficiently. This approach is commonly referred to as bulkifying your code and helps in staying within Salesforce governor limits.

Here's an example of how you can structure to follow. This code dynamically queries for Account records created in the last month and then retrieves associated Contact records, updating the Title field on those Contact records.

```
List<Contact> contactsToUpdate = new List<Contact>();

// Query for Account records created in the last month
Date lastMonthStartDate = Date.today().addMonths(-1).toStartOfMonth();
Date lastMonthEndDate = Date.today().toStartOfMonth();
Set<Id> accountIds = new Set<Id>();
for (Account acc : [SELECT Id FROM Account WHERE CreatedDate >=
:lastMonthStartDate AND CreatedDate < :lastMonthEndDate]) {
    accountIds.add(acc.Id);
}

// Query related Contacts for the dynamically obtained Account Ids
// outside the loop
List<Contact> relatedContacts = [SELECT Id, Name, Title FROM Contact WHERE
AccountId IN :accountIds];

// Update the Title field on contacts
for (Contact con : relatedContacts) {
Contact updatedContact = new Contact(Id = con.Id);
    updatedContact.Title = 'Updated Value';
    contactsToUpdate.add(updatedContact);
}
```

```
// Perform bulk update if there are contacts to update
if (!contactsToUpdate.isEmpty()) {
    update contactsToUpdate;
}
```

1. The first SOQL query retrieves Account records created in the last month and adds their Id values to the accountIds set. This query is placed outside the loop, ensuring that only one query is executed regardless of the number of Account records.

2. The second SOQL query retrieves Contact records based on the dynamically obtained Account Ids. Again, this query is placed outside the loop, preventing unnecessary queries inside the loop.

3. The subsequent loop updates the Title field on the queried Contact records, and the final bulk update is performed outside the loop if there are contacts to update.

By using SOSL queries with Maps, you can avoid nested loops and efficiently retrieve and work with related records. This approach can help improve performance and avoid hitting CPU limits in your Apex code.

Here's an example to illustrate this approach. The code starts by defining a list of SObject types (searchTypes), which includes Account and Contact. It initializes a map (relatedRecordsMap) to store related records based on their SObjectType.

```
List<SObjectType> searchTypes = new List<SObjectType>
{Account.SObjectType, Contact.SObjectType};
Map<SObjectType, List<SObject>> relatedRecordsMap = new Map<SObjectType,
List<SObject>>();

// Build the SOSL query
List<List<SObject>> searchResults = [FIND '{search term}'
RETURNING Account(Name), Contact(Name)];

// Iterate over the search results and populate the Map
for (Integer i = 0; i < searchResults.size(); i++) {
    List<SObject> records = searchResults[i];
    SObjectType objectType = searchTypes[i];
    relatedRecordsMap.put(objectType, records);
}
```

```
// Access the related records from the Map
List<SObject> accountRecords = relatedRecordsMap.get(Account.SObjectType);
List<SObject> contactRecords = relatedRecordsMap.get(Contact.SObjectType);

// Perform operations on the related records
```

1. The SOSL query is designed to search for a specified term across both Account and Contact objects in a single query. This is more efficient than running separate queries for each object type.

2. The use of a map (relatedRecordsMap) allows to organize the related records by their SObjectType. This structure provides a convenient way to access and work with the records for each object type without the need for additional nested loops.

3. Bulkifying your code by using SOSL and maps helps in avoiding CPU limits. This is important in Salesforce Apex, where governor limits are enforced to ensure the efficient use of resources.

4. By minimizing the number of queries and efficiently organizing related records, the overall performance of your Apex code is likely to improve. This becomes especially crucial when dealing with large datasets or executing code in a bulk context.

By using Limits.getHeapSize and implementing pagination, you can effectively manage the heap size and avoid hitting heap size limits in your Apex code. The same approach can be applied to SOQL and SOSL queries as well.

Here's an example of using Limits.getHeapSize and pagination limit of 100 to check the heap size before and after executing the SOQL query:

```
// Set the batch size for pagination
Integer batchSize = 100;

// Set the initial offset for pagination
Id lastRecordId = null;

// Initialize a list to store the retrieved records
List<Account> accounts = new List<Account>();
```

```
while (true) {
    // Check the heap size before executing the query
    Long startHeapSize = Limits.getHeapSize();

    // Query records with pagination using WHERE and ORDER BY
    List<Account> queryResults = [
        SELECT Id, Name FROM Account
        WHERE Id > :lastRecordId
        ORDER BY Id
        LIMIT :batchSize
    ];

    // Check the heap size after adding records
    Long endHeapSize = Limits.getHeapSize();

    // Check if adding the current batch exceeds the heap size limit
    if (endHeapSize - startHeapSize >= Limits.getLimitHeapSize()) {
        // Perform necessary operations when approaching heap size limit

        // ...

        // Break the loop to avoid exceeding the heap size limit

        break;
    }

    // Add the retrieved records to the list
    accounts.addAll(queryResults);

    // Break the loop if all records have been retrieved
    if (queryResults.size() < batchSize) {
        break;
    }

    // Update the last record ID for the next batch
    lastRecordId = queryResults[queryResults.size() - 1].Id;
}
```

```
// Process the retrieved records
for (Account account : accounts) {
    // Perform necessary operations on each account
}
```

1. The code checks the heap size before and after executing the SOQL query using Limits.getHeapSize. If adding the current batch of records would exceed the heap size limit, the code performs necessary operations and breaks the loop to avoid exceeding the limit.

2. The code implements pagination to retrieve records in chunks, preventing issues related to hitting the query row limit. This is essential when dealing with large datasets, as Salesforce imposes limits on the number of records you can retrieve in a single query.

3. The approach of using Limits.getHeapSize and pagination is applicable to both SOQL and SOSL queries. It's a good practice to monitor and manage the heap size whenever you are dealing with data retrieval and processing in Apex.

In Salesforce, you can use both Developer Console and Workbench `https://workbench.developerforce.com/login.php` as additional web-based application provided by Salesforce to execute SOQL and SOSL queries. Workbench is a versatile, user-friendly tool for various tasks, while Developer Console is focused on code development and debugging but includes query capabilities for developers working within that environment. Choose the tool that best aligns with your specific needs and workflow.

CHAPTER 7

Triggers and Bulk Processing

7.1 Triggers and Their Execution Context

Apex triggers are a powerful feature in Salesforce that allow you to execute custom logic before or after records are inserted, updated, or deleted in the database. They are associated with SObjects, which can be either standard objects such as Account, Contact, Opportunity, etc. or custom objects created to meet specific business requirements.

Triggers are used to perform actions or enforce business rules whenever these events occur. They provide a way to customize and extend the functionality of Salesforce.

The execution context refers to the environment in which an Apex trigger is executed. It includes various aspects such as the order of execution, the record or records being processed, and the values of the fields being modified.

Triggers in Salesforce offer several key features and capabilities:

- *Custom Logic*: Triggers allow developers to write custom logic in Apex code to perform specific actions or enforce business rules when records are created, updated, or deleted.

- *Data Validation*: Triggers can be used to validate data before it is saved to the database. This ensures that the data meets specific criteria or follows certain business rules.

- *Record Enrichment*: Triggers can enrich records by automatically populating fields or performing calculations based on other field values or external data sources.

© Konstantin Kapitanov 2024
K. Kapitanov, *Salesforce Developer I Certification*, Certification Study Companion Series,
https://doi.org/10.1007/979-8-8688-0300-0_7

- *Related Record Updates*: Triggers can update related records when a specific event occurs on a record. For example, when a new Opportunity is created, a trigger can automatically create related Task records for follow-up activities.

- *Workflow Automation*: Triggers can automate complex workflows by performing multiple actions based on specific conditions or events.

- *Integration with External Systems*: Triggers can integrate with external systems or APIs to perform actions or retrieve data from external sources.

- *Debugging and Logging*: Triggers can be debugged and logged to track their execution and troubleshoot any issues.

There are two types of triggers in Salesforce:

1. *Before Triggers*: Before triggers are used to update or validate record values before they are saved to the database. They allow developers to modify data before it is committed to the database. Before triggers are commonly used for data validation and enrichment purposes.

2. *After Triggers*: After triggers are used to access field values that are set by the system after the record is saved to the database. They allow developers to perform actions based on the updated values of the record. After triggers are commonly used for tasks that require access to the updated record data, such as sending notifications or updating related records.

A trigger is defined using the trigger keyword, followed by the trigger name and the object on which the trigger operates. You specify the trigger event like before insert and the trigger code block as in the following example.

Let us create a new trigger on the contact object. Go to Setup ➤ Object Manager tab ➤ Contact ➤ Triggers, and click the "New" button.

```
trigger ContactTrigger on Contact (before insert) {
    for (Contact con : Trigger.new) {
        // Set standard field values for the newly inserted Contact records
```

```
        con.firstname= 'Max';
        con.LastName = 'Blank';
    }
}
```

Now when you insert new Contact records, this trigger ensures that the FirstName is set to "Max" and the LastName is set to "Blank" before the records are actually inserted into the Salesforce database. You can test the Apex trigger in your Salesforce environment by creating the new contact.

Trigger events indicate when the trigger code should execute in relation to the database operation. Common trigger events include *(before insert), (before update), (before delete), (after insert), (after update), (after delete), and (after undelete)*.

When multiple triggers are defined for the same object and event, Salesforce determines the order in which they are executed. The order of execution primary include but not limited to:

1. System Validation Rules

   - Salesforce performs system validation, such as verifying that all required fields have a non-null value and that unique fields have unique values.

2. Before Triggers

   - All before triggers are executed.

   - Custom validation rules are executed.

3. After Triggers

   - All after triggers are executed.

4. Assignment Rules

   - If the record was updated in the transaction, assignment rules are executed.

5. Auto-Response Rules

   - If the record was created and meets the criteria for auto-response rules, these rules are executed.

6. Workflow Rules

    • Workflow rules are executed.

7. Processes and Flows

    • Processes and Flows are executed.

8. Escalation Rules

    • If the record is associated with an entitlement and meets the criteria for escalation rules, these rules are executed.

9. DML Operations to Database

    • Commit DML operations to Database.

10. Post-Commit Logic

    • Any post-commit logic, such as sending emails or updating external systems, is executed.

It's important to note that the execution order can be influenced by factors such as the type of operation being performed and whether the trigger is defined at the object or field level.

7.2 Create Triggers with Context Variables

Context variables in Apex are special variables that provide information about the current execution context of your code. They contain data related to the environment in which your code is running, such as trigger events, records being processed, and user information. These context variables help you understand and respond to different situations during code execution.

In the context of Apex triggers, there are several context variables that are commonly used to access information about the trigger's execution. Here are the main context variables and their purposes:

Trigger.new and Trigger.old

These context variables are used to provide access to the new and old versions of records in a trigger:

- *Trigger.new*: Returns a list of the new versions of the sObject records. This list is available in insert, update, and undelete triggers.

- *Trigger.old*: Returns a list of the old versions of the sObject records. This list is available in update and delete triggers.

These context variables allow developers to compare the old and new values of records and perform actions based on the changes. For example, in an update trigger, you can use Trigger.new and Trigger.old to identify which fields have changed and take appropriate actions.

Imagine you want to enforce a validation rule during the conversion of leads in Salesforce. Specifically, you want to ensure that converted leads have a certain minimum lead rating before they can be converted. You can use the Trigger.new context variable to access the leads being converted and perform the validation.

Go to Setup ➤ Object Manager tab ➤ Lead ➤ Triggers, and click the "New" button.

```
trigger LeadConversionValidation on Lead (before update) {
    List<Lead> leadsToConvert = new List<Lead>();

    // Iterate through the leads being updated (converted)
    for (Lead lead : Trigger.new) {
        if (lead.IsConverted) {
            leadsToConvert.add(lead);
        }
    }

    // Check lead scores before conversion
    for (Lead convertedLead : leadsToConvert) {
        if (convertedLead.Rating != 'Hot') {
            convertedLead.addError
            ('Leads must have a lead rating of "Hot" to be converted.');
        }
    }
}
```

In this example:

- The trigger is set to execute before update on the Lead object.

- The trigger iterates through the leads in the Trigger.new collection.

- If a lead is being converted (IsConverted is true), it's added to the leadsToConvert list.

- Another loop checks the lead rating of the leads to be converted.

- If a lead's rating is not "Hot," an error message is added to the lead using the addError method. This prevents the conversion from proceeding.

This use case example demonstrates how you can use the Trigger.new context variable to access and manipulate the records being processed in an Apex trigger. By leveraging this variable, you can enforce custom business rules and data validation during various database operations.

Now, if you try to set any value other than "Hot" in the Rating field when converting Leads, you will get an error "Validation error on Lead: Leads must have a lead rating of 'Hot' to be converted."

Please note that Trigger.new and Trigger.old cannot be used in Apex DML operations. These context variables are used to access the records that caused the trigger to fire, but they cannot be used to perform DML operations such as insert, update, or delete on the records. Therefore, if you need to perform DML operations on the records, you should create a separate list or map variable and perform the DML operations on that variable instead of using Trigger.new or Trigger.old.

Trigger.newMap and Trigger.oldMap

They are context variables that provide access to the new and old versions of records in a trigger, represented as maps that associate record IDs with their corresponding records. They are useful for efficiently accessing records and comparing old and new values.

- *Trigger.newMap*: Returns a map of record IDs to the new versions of the sObject records. This map is available in before update, after insert, after update, and after undelete triggers.

- *Trigger.oldMap*: Returns a map of record IDs to the old versions of the sObject records. This map is available in before update, after update, before delete, and after delete triggers.

Trigger.size

The Trigger.size variable in Apex triggers is used to determine the total number of records in a trigger invocation, including both old and new records. It provides the count of records that caused the trigger to fire.

Here are a few reasons why Trigger.size is commonly used in Apex triggers:

- *Bulk Processing*: Apex triggers are designed to handle bulk operations, where multiple records are processed simultaneously. By using Trigger.size, you can perform validations or actions based on the number of records being processed. For example, you can enforce limits on the number of records that can be inserted or updated at once. It allows you also to process records in batches, which can help you stay within Salesforce governor limits as in the next example here.

- *Governor Limits*: Salesforce imposes various governor limits to ensure the efficient use of resources. These limits include the number of records processed in a single transaction. By using Trigger.size, you can monitor and control the number of records being processed to avoid hitting these limits.

- *Recursion Handling*: In some cases, triggers can cause recursion, where a trigger invokes itself repeatedly. By using Trigger.size, you can implement logic to handle recursion and prevent infinite loops. For example, you can set a static variable to track the number of times the trigger has executed and use Trigger.size to check if it's the first execution or a subsequent one.

It's important to note that Trigger.size represents the total number of records in a trigger invocation, not just the number of records being inserted or updated. Therefore, it can be used to handle various scenarios and implement logic based on the number of records involved.

Suppose you want to track changes made to a specific custom field on an object. Whenever that field is modified, you want to create a history record that captures the old and new values of the field. You can use the Trigger.oldMap context variable to access the previous values of the field and compare them with the new values in Trigger.new.

Step 1: Go to Setup ➤ Object Manager tab. Click the "Create" button ➤ Custom Object. Create new custom object with name "History" and save. After creating the new object, the API name will be set automatically to History__c.

Step 2: Create four new custom fields on the History__c custom object as follows by going to Setup ➤ Object Manager tab. Click History object ➤ Fields and Relationships on the left menu. Click "New" button to create new field.

Object_Id: Lookup to the Lead object
Field_Name: Text field to store the API name of the field being tracked
Old_Value: Text field to store the old value of the tracked field
New_Value: Text field to store the new value of the tracked field

Step 3: Go to Setup ➤ Type Tabs in the search field on the left menu in the area Custom Object Tabs. Click the button "New" to add and make new created customer object History__c visible in your Salesforce App Launcher.

Step 4: Go to Setup ➤ Object Manager tab ➤ Lead ➤ Triggers, and click the "New" button.

```
// This trigger captures changes in the 'Rating' field for Lead records.
// It leverages Trigger.size for efficient bulk processing.

trigger FieldChangeTracking on Lead (after update) {
    // List to store History__c records for field changes
    List<History__c> historyRecords = new List<History__c>();

    // Field API name to track changes
    String fieldToTrack = 'Rating';

    // Iterate through the updated records using Trigger.size
    for (Integer i = 0; i < Trigger.size; i++) {
        // Retrieve new and old versions of the Lead record
        Lead newLead = Trigger.new[i];
        Lead oldLead = Trigger.old[i];

        // Compare old and new values of the specified field ('Rating')
        if (oldLead != null && newLead.get(fieldToTrack) != oldLead.
        get(fieldToTrack)) {
            // Create a new History__c record to capture the field change
            History__c history = new History__c(
                Object_Id__c = newLead.Id,
                Field_Name__c = fieldToTrack,
                Old_Value__c = String.valueOf(oldLead.get(fieldToTrack)),
                New_Value__c = String.valueOf(newLead.get(fieldToTrack))
            );
```

```
        // Add the history record to the list
        historyRecords.add(history);
    }
}

// Insert history records into the database if changes were detected
if (!historyRecords.isEmpty()) {
    insert historyRecords;
}
}
```

In this example:

- The trigger is set to execute after update on the Lead object.

- The trigger iterates through the records in Trigger.newMap.

- For each record, it retrieves the corresponding old version from Trigger.oldMap using the record's ID.

- It compares the old and new values of the specified field *Rating*.

- If the field value has changed, it creates a new History__c record to capture the change.

- The history records, accumulated using Trigger.size, are then inserted into the database.

By using Trigger.oldMap in this example, you can access the previous values of the records before the update and compare them with the new values. This allows you to implement advanced logic that reacts to specific changes in your data and performs related actions.

Now, you can change the values in the Rating field after creating new leads on your Lead object and track the value changes in the newly created customer object's History__c.

Trigger.isInsert, Trigger.isUpdate, Trigger.isDelete, Trigger.isUndelete

These are context variables that provide information about the type of operation that caused the trigger to fire. These variables are contained in the System.Trigger class and are commonly used to control the flow of logic within triggers.

- *Trigger.isInsert*: Returns true if the trigger was fired due to an insert operation. This includes inserts performed through the Salesforce user interface, Apex code, or the API.

- *Trigger.isUpdate*: Returns true if the trigger was fired due to an update operation. This includes updates performed through the Salesforce user interface, Apex code, or the API.

- *Trigger.isDelete*: Returns true if the trigger was fired due to a delete operation. This includes deletions performed through the Salesforce user interface, Apex code, or the API.

- *Trigger.isUndelete*: Returns true if the trigger was fired after a record is recovered from the Recycle Bin. This includes undelete operations performed through the Salesforce user interface, Apex code, or the API.

In the following example, we want to automate the creation of an opportunity record whenever a new account is inserted into Salesforce. You can use the Trigger.isInsert context variable to determine if the trigger event is an insert and then create a related opportunity record.

Go to Setup ➤ Object Manager tab ➤ Account ➤ Triggers, and click the "New" button.

```
trigger CreateOpportunityOnAccountInsert on Account (after insert) {
    List<Opportunity> newOpportunities = new List<Opportunity>();

    for (Account acc : Trigger.new) {
        if (Trigger.isInsert) {
            // Create an opportunity with account information
            Opportunity newOpportunity = new Opportunity(
                Name = 'New Opportunity',
                StageName = 'Prospecting',
                CloseDate = Date.today().addDays(30), // Set the close date
                as needed
                AccountId = acc.Id
            );
            newOpportunities.add(newOpportunity);
        }
    }
```

```
    // Insert the new opportunities
    if (!newOpportunities.isEmpty()) {
        insert newOpportunities;
    }
}
```

In this example:

- The trigger is set to execute after insert on the Account object.

- The trigger iterates through the new account records in Trigger.new.

- The trigger uses Trigger.isInsert to confirm that the event is an insert operation.

- For each new account, a corresponding opportunity is created with a default name, StageName, CloseDate, and the account's ID is associated.

- The new opportunity is inserted into the database.

By using this Trigger.isInsert example, you ensure that the opportunity creation logic only runs when new accounts are inserted.

Trigger.isBefore, Trigger.isAfter

These context variables provide information about the timing of the trigger execution. These variables are contained in the System.Trigger class and are commonly used to control the flow of logic within triggers.

- *Trigger.isBefore*: Returns true if the trigger was fired before any record was saved. This variable is often used to perform actions or validations before the records are saved.

- *Trigger.isAfter*: Returns true if the trigger was fired after all records were saved. This variable is often used to perform actions or calculations after the records have been saved.

The following example is designed to execute after a Contact record is updated. It monitors changes in the Email field of Contact records and creates Chatter feed items for Contacts where the email has been updated.

```
trigger ContactEmailUpdate on Contact (after update) {
    // Check if the trigger is running after the update operation
    if (Trigger.isAfter) {
        // Create a list to hold the updated contacts
        List<Contact> updatedContacts = new List<Contact>();

        // Iterate through the updated contacts
        for (Contact contact : Trigger.new) {
            // Check if the email field has been changed
            if (contact.Email != Trigger.oldMap.get(contact.Id).Email) {
                // Add the updated contact to the list
                updatedContacts.add(contact);
            }
        }

        // Check if there are any updated contacts
        if (!updatedContacts.isEmpty()) {
            // Create a Chatter feed item for each updated contact
            List<FeedItem> feedItems = new List<FeedItem>();

            for (Contact contact : updatedContacts) {
                // Create the Chatter feed item with the new
                // email information
                FeedItem feedItem = new FeedItem();
                feedItem.ParentId = contact.Id;
                feedItem.Body = 'The email for the contact ' + contact.Name
                    + ' has been updated to ' + contact.Email;
                feedItem.Type = 'TextPost';

                feedItems.add(feedItem);
            }

            // Insert the Chatter feed items
            insert feedItems;
        }
    }
}
```

In this example:

- It checks if it is running after the update operation if Trigger.isAfter.

- It creates a list updatedContacts to hold the Contacts that have been updated.

- It iterates through the Contacts in Trigger.new the updated Contacts and compares the new Email value with the old Email value from Trigger.oldMap.

- If the Email has changed, the Contact is added to the updatedContacts list.

- For each updated Contact, a Chatter feed item is created.

IsExecuting

Common use cases for this variable include

- *Avoiding Recursive Triggers*: You might use isExecuting to prevent a trigger from firing recursively.

- *Handling Trigger Logic in Utility Classes*: Utility classes that are called from triggers might use isExecuting to adjust their behavior based on whether they are invoked within a trigger.

- *Logging and Debugging*: Logging or debugging statements might be conditionally included based on whether the code is running in a trigger context.

Having multiple triggers on the same object can lead to unpredictable execution order. Like recursion often occurs when a trigger performs an action that causes another trigger to fire. The problem of recursive triggers in Apex occurs when a trigger on a Salesforce object performs an action that causes the trigger to be invoked again, resulting in an infinite loop. This can lead to performance issues, governor limit errors, and unexpected behavior in your application.

To avoid recursive triggers in Apex, you can implement the following approaches as in the following example:

1. *Static Boolean Variable*: Create a static Boolean variable, and use it to track whether the trigger has already been executed. Set the variable to true before executing the trigger logic, and reset it to false after the logic is completed. Check the value of this variable at the beginning of the trigger to prevent recursion.

2. *Trigger Context Variables*: Use the Trigger context variables, such as Trigger.isExecuting and Trigger.new, to control the execution of the trigger. By checking these variables, you can determine if the trigger is being executed for the first time or if it is being called recursively.

In this example, we'll create a trigger on the Account object that updates the Description field. The static Boolean variable will be used to prevent recursion.

```
trigger AccountTrigger on Account (before update) {
    // Static Boolean variable to track trigger execution
    private static Boolean isExecuting = false;

    // Check if the trigger is already executing to avoid recursion
    if (isExecuting) {
        return;
    }

    // Set the trigger as executing to prevent recursion
    isExecuting = true;

    // Get the updated accounts
    List<Account> updatedAccounts = Trigger.new;

    // Update the Description field for each account
    for (Account acc : updatedAccounts) {
        acc.Description = 'Trigger Updated';
    }

    // Reset the trigger execution status
    isExecuting = false;
}
```

- Static Boolean Variable is used to track whether the trigger is currently executing. It's marked as static so that its value persists across trigger invocations.

- The purpose of this variable is to prevent recursion. If the trigger is already executing, it skips the logic to avoid an infinite loop.

- The trigger checks if it's already executing (if (isExecuting)). If it is, the trigger returns early without performing any further actions. This check helps to prevent recursive trigger execution.

- The trigger then proceeds to process the records in Trigger.new. In this case, it iterates over the updated Account records.

- For each Account in the trigger, it sets the Description field to "Trigger Updated". This is a simple example of modifying the records before they are saved to the database.

- After processing the records, the trigger resets the isExecuting variable to false. This step is important to allow future trigger executions to proceed.

It's important to carefully design and test your triggers to avoid recursion and ensure proper functionality. By implementing these practices, you can prevent recursive triggers and maintain the integrity and performance of your Salesforce application. Then usage of a single trigger per object is a best practice in Salesforce Apex because it promotes code organization, maintainability, and avoids unnecessary complexity. A single trigger ensures that your logic executes in a predictable sequence, which can be important for enforcing business rules.

7.3 Bulk Processing for Large Datasets

Collections like lists, sets, and maps are essential for bulk processing. They allow you to group and manipulate records efficiently. Fetch required data outside the loop and use collections to match and process records. Utilize bulk DML operations to update, insert, or delete multiple records in a single transaction.

In the following example, the trigger creates subsidiary accounts for new parent accounts where the BillingAddress fields are null. The provided trigger is designed to handle bulk processing efficiently.

```
trigger CreateSubsidiaryAccounts on Account (after insert) {

    List<Account> newSubsidiaryAccounts = new List<Account>();

    for (Account acc : Trigger.new) {
        // Check if BillingAddress components are empty for new accounts
        if (acc.BillingStreet == null && acc.BillingCity == null &&
        acc.BillingState == null && acc.BillingPostalCode == null &&
        acc.BillingCountry == null) {
            // Create a new subsidiary account
            newSubsidiaryAccounts.add(new Account(
                Name = 'Subsidiary Account', // Adjust as needed
                ParentId = acc.Id
            ));
        }
    }

    // Insert new subsidiary accounts outside the loop
    if (newSubsidiaryAccounts.size() > 0) {
        insert newSubsidiaryAccounts;
    }
}
```

1. *It Operates on Collections*: The loop processes multiple accounts in a single iteration, which is more efficient than processing one record at a time.

2. *It Doesn't Perform DML Operations Inside the Loop*: The creation of subsidiary accounts is collected in a list (newSubsidiaryAccounts), and the DML operation (insert) is performed outside the loop, which helps avoid hitting governor limits on DML statements.

3. *The Trigger Is Focused on a Specific Task*: creating subsidiary accounts without unnecessary complexity, making it more maintainable.

To ensure its effectiveness with bulk data, always test triggers in a sandbox environment with representative data volumes before deploying to production.

Note! For small triggers with simple logic, like the examples we discussed for demonstration purposes earlier, it is acceptable to write the logic directly inside the trigger without creating a separate class. This approach can be convenient and straightforward, particularly for small-scale or one-off triggers.

But it's important to keep in mind that as your codebase grows and becomes more complex, it is generally recommended by following best practices to separate the trigger logic into a separate class. This helps improve code maintainability, reusability, and testability.

Here's how you can create a separate Apex class to provide the same functionality as in our last example but to handle the logic for creating subsidiary accounts separately.

Step 1: Create a new Apex class *createSubsidiaryAccounts* in Developer Console:

```
public class SubsidiaryAccountHandler {
    private static Boolean isExecuting = false;

    public static void createSubsidiaryAccounts(List<Account>
    newAccounts) {
        if (!isExecuting) {
            isExecuting = true;

            List<Account> newSubsidiaryAccounts = new List<Account>();

            for (Account acc : newAccounts) {
// Check if BillingAddress components are empty for new accounts
                if (acc.BillingStreet == null && acc.BillingCity ==
                null && acc.BillingState == null && acc.BillingPostalCode ==
                null && acc.BillingCountry == null) {
                    // Create a new subsidiary account
                    newSubsidiaryAccounts.add(new Account(
                        Name = 'Subsidiary Account', // Adjust as needed
                        ParentId = acc.Id
                    ));
                }
            }
        }
```

```
        // Insert new subsidiary accounts outside the loop
        if (newSubsidiaryAccounts.size() > 0) {
            insert newSubsidiaryAccounts;
        }

        isExecuting = false;
    }
  }
}
```

Step 2: Go to Setup ➤ Object Manager tab ➤ Account ➤ Triggers ➤ CreateSubsidiaryAccounts and click the "Edit" button.

```
trigger CreateSubsidiaryAccounts on Account (after insert) {
    SubsidiaryAccountHandler.createSubsidiaryAccounts(Trigger.new);
}
```

Our CreateSubsidiaryAccounts trigger has been updated now. If you need to perform similar logic in another context, you can easily reuse the SubsidiaryAccountHandler class.

CHAPTER 8

Access Control and Permissions

8.1 Execution Context

In Apex, there are two types of execution contexts such as system execution context and user execution context. User execution context is when a user clicks a button or link, for example, that executes Apex code. When a system event or process executes Apex code, a system execution context is created. Apex does not enforce object-level and field-level permissions in system mode by default, but the new ***AccessLevel class*** represents the two modes in which Apex runs database operations. You can use this class to define the execution mode as user mode or system mode. The key difference between the previously used WITH SECURITY_ENFORCED keyword and the new AccessLevel class is that the AccessLevel class allows you to specify the mode of execution as either user mode or system mode. In user mode, the code respects the field-level security (FLS), object permissions, and sharing rules of the running user. On the other hand, in system mode, the class sharing keywords control the sharing rules.

The WITH SECURITY_ENFORCED keyword, introduced earlier, allows you to enforce field-level security (FLS) and object permissions in SOQL queries. It ensures that the query results only include the fields and records that the running user has access to. However, it does not provide the ability to run the code in user mode or system mode.

With the new AccessLevel class, you can explicitly define the execution mode as user mode or system mode for database operations. This allows you to run the code with the appropriate permissions and sharing rules based on the context in which it is being executed.

© Konstantin Kapitanov 2024
K. Kapitanov, *Salesforce Developer I Certification*, Certification Study Companion Series,
https://doi.org/10.1007/979-8-8688-0300-0_8

User Context:

```
AccessLevel userMode = AccessLevel.USER_MODE;
List<Opportunity> opportunitiesUserMode = Database.query
('SELECT Name, Amount FROM Opportunity WITH USER_MODE');
System.debug('Opportunities in User Mode: ' + opportunitiesUserMode);
```

System Context:

```
AccessLevel systemMode = AccessLevel.SYSTEM_MODE;
List<Opportunity> opportunitiesSystemMode = Database.query
('SELECT Name, Amount FROM Opportunity WITH SYSTEM_MODE');
System.debug('Opportunities in System Mode: ' + opportunitiesSystemMode);
```

The preceding code, you can check in Developer Console. But when you try to execute systemMode code in Developer Console will get an error "System. SecurityException: Cannot use SYSTEM_MODE access level in anonymous execution of Apex." That is because you would need to execute the code within a proper context, such as a deployed Apex class or a trigger, where security checks and access controls are in place.

Please note that the debug output will depend on the specific data available in your Salesforce organization. Make sure to check the debug logs to see the actual results returned by the queries.

8.2 Using the Schema.DescribeFieldResult Class

To enforce object and field-level permissions, you can call the isAccessible(), isCreateable(), isUpdateable(), or isDeletable() methods of the Schema. DescribeSObjectResult class to verify whether the current user has read, create, or update access to an object. These methods can be used in any context and are not limited to the system execution context. They are commonly used in scenarios where you need dynamically adapt your code based on the permissions of the running user has specific on a field or object. You use them to make decisions based on individual permissions. Like to check if the current user has access to an object, you can use the isAccessible method. This method returns a value indicating whether the object is accessible to the user.

However, it is important to note that you need to include all the fields you want to access in your SOQL query.

Here's an example that demonstrates how to check field accessibility and retrieve the necessary fields in a query:

```
List<Opportunity> opportunities = [SELECT Name, Amount, StageName FROM
Opportunity];
List<Opportunity> sanitizedOpportunities = new List<Opportunity>();

for (Opportunity opp : opportunities) { if
    (Schema.sObjectType.Opportunity.fields.StageName.isAccessible
    () && opp.StageName == 'Prospecting') {
        Opportunity sanitizedOpp = new Opportunity();
        sanitizedOpp.Name = opp.Name;
        sanitizedOpp.Amount = opp.Amount;
        sanitizedOpportunities.add(sanitizedOpp);
    }
}

System.debug('Sanitized Opportunities: ' + sanitizedOpportunities);
```

In the given code snippet, we start by querying Opportunities from Salesforce, specifically selecting the Name, Amount, and StageName fields.

To ascertain the accessibility of the StageName field, we utilize the isAccessible() method from the Schema.DescribeFieldResult class. This method helps confirm whether the current user has read access to the StageName field.

The condition opp.StageName == 'Prospecting' is employed to identify Opportunities that are in the "Prospecting" stage. If the StageName field is accessible and the Opportunity is in the specified stage, we proceed to create a new Opportunity object called sanitizedOpp. This new object is then populated with the Name and Amount fields from the original Opportunity (opp).

The Opportunities meeting the "Prospecting" stage criteria are accumulated in the sanitizedOpportunities list. To conclude, we utilize the System.debug() statement to display the contents of the sanitizedOpportunities list, providing visibility into Opportunities that fulfill the specified condition.

8.3 Implementing Security. stripInaccessible() Method

This method allows you to filter records based on the permissions of the current user. It can be used to remove fields and objects that the user does not have access to across a set of records. It´s often used when dealing with collections of records like a list of SObjects where you want to filter out fields that the user does not have access to. This method could be useful to remove inaccessible fields from sObjects before DML operation to avoid exceptions.

In the provided example, you are using Security.stripInaccessible to filter out inaccessible fields, modifying a field, and then performing a DML operation to update the modified records on account object.

```
List<Account> accounts = [SELECT Id, Name, AccountNumber, Description FROM
Account LIMIT 2];

// Add SObjectAccessDecision to strip inaccessible records
SObjectAccessDecision decision = Security.stripInaccessible
(AccessType.READABLE, accounts);

// Retrieve the sanitized account records
List<Account> sanitizedAccounts = decision.getRecords();

// Modify the Name field of the first account in the list
if (!sanitizedAccounts.isEmpty()) {
    Account firstAccount = sanitizedAccounts[0];
    firstAccount.Name = 'New Updated Name';
}

// Perform DML to update the modified account
if (!sanitizedAccounts.isEmpty()) {
    update sanitizedAccounts;
}

// Retrieve the updated account records
List<Account> updatedAccounts = [SELECT Id, Name, AccountNumber,
Description FROM Account WHERE Id IN :sanitizedAccounts];
```

```
// Add debug statement to display the updated account records
System.debug('Updated Accounts: ' + updatedAccounts);
```

This code retrieves a list of accounts from the database and then uses the Security. stripInaccessible() method to remove any inaccessible records based on the READABLE access type.

The sanitized account records are stored in the sanitizedAccounts list. The code then modifies the Name field of the first account in the sanitizedAccounts list, setting it to "New Updated Name". Next, a DML update operation is performed on the sanitizedAccounts list to persist the changes to the database.

The code then queries the updated account records from the database, including the Id, Name, AccountNumber, and Description fields for the updated accounts. Finally, a debug statement is used to display the updated account records in the debug logs.

The use of Security.stripInaccessible() is important as it ensures that only accessible records are included in the sanitizedAccounts list. This helps maintain data security by filtering out any inaccessible records before performing the update operation. By using this method, the code respects the user's access privileges and ensures that updates are only made to records that the user has the necessary permissions to modify.

CHAPTER 9

Testing

9.1 How to Write Test Cases

Unit tests in Apex are written using the Apex testing framework, which provides a set of classes and methods specifically designed for testing Apex code. These tests are typically written by developers to validate the functionality of their code and ensure that it meets the desired requirements.

In Salesforce, before moving the code to production, a minimum of 75% code coverage is required. This means that at least 75% of your Apex code must be covered by unit tests. Code coverage is a measure of how much of your Apex code is executed during the running of your tests. Each line of code that is executed during a test is considered as covered, while lines that are not executed are considered as uncovered. To check the overall code coverage in Salesforce, you can go in Developer Console to the Tests tab and check the Overall Code Coverage panel, which displays the code coverage percentage for every Apex class in the organization that has been tested. Alternatively you can go with Salesforce user interface to Setup and then to Apex Test Execution.

The @isTest annotation in Apex is used to define a class or method as a test class or test method, respectively. This annotation is used to indicate that the code within the annotated class or method is intended for testing purposes and should not be counted against the organization's limit for Apex code. Test classes and methods are used to verify the behavior and functionality of Apex classes and triggers. They are executed separately from the main code and are used to ensure that the code is working as expected. Test methods take no arguments and commit no data to the database.

Positive and negative tests are two different types of tests used to validate the behavior of a system or a specific piece of code. Positive tests typically cover scenarios where valid inputs are provided, and the system is expected to produce the correct output or behavior. Examples of positive tests include

© Konstantin Kapitanov 2024
K. Kapitanov, *Salesforce Developer I Certification*, Certification Study Companion Series,
https://doi.org/10.1007/979-8-8688-0300-0_9

- Testing a login functionality with valid credentials

- Verifying that a calculation method returns the correct result with valid input values

- Checking that a form validation process accepts valid data

Negative tests are crucial to ensuring the system's robustness and its ability to handle errors gracefully. Examples of negative tests include

- Providing invalid login credentials and verifying that the system rejects them

- Testing a calculation method with invalid or out-of-range input values and ensuring it handles the errors appropriately

- Entering invalid data into a form and checking that the validation process detects and rejects it

Write unit tests in Developer Edition or a sandbox to ensure that each unit of code like class or method works as expected. Now, we will revisit the first trigger example *ContactTrigger* from Chapter 5 and create test class by using three different assert methods.

Step 1: Open Developer Console ➤ File ➤ New ➤ Apex Class *"TestContactTrigger"* ➤ Insert the code

```
@isTest
private class TestContactTrigger {

    @isTest
    static void testContactTriggerWithSystemEquals() {
        // Test case using System.assertEquals

        // Create a new contact without setting FirstName and LastName

        Contact testContact = new Contact();
        insert testContact;

        // Retrieve the contact from the database to ensure trigger
        // logic is applied
        Contact insertedContact = [SELECT Id, FirstName, LastName FROM
        Contact WHERE Id = :testContact.Id];
```

```
    // Verify that the trigger correctly set the standard field values
    // using System.assertEquals
          System.assertEquals('Max', insertedContact.FirstName,
          'FirstName should be set to "Max".');
          System.assertEquals('Blank', insertedContact.LastName,
          'LastName should be set to "Blank".');
}

@isTest
static void testContactTriggerWithSystemAssertNotEquals() {
    // Test case using System.assertNotEquals

    // Create a new contact without setting FirstName and LastName

    Contact testContact = new Contact();
    insert testContact;

    // Retrieve the contact from the database to ensure trigger logic
    // is applied
    Contact insertedContact = [SELECT Id, FirstName, LastName FROM
    Contact WHERE Id = :testContact.Id];

    // Verify that the trigger did not set unexpected values using
    // System.assertNotEquals
    System.assertNotEquals('Unexpected Value', insertedContact.FirstName,
    'FirstName should not be "Unexpected Value".');
    System.assertNotEquals('Unexpected Value', insertedContact.LastName,
    'LastName should not be "Unexpected Value".');
}

@isTest
static void testContactTriggerWithSystemAssert() {
    // Test case using System.assert

    // Create a new contact without setting FirstName and LastName
    Contact testContact = new Contact();
    insert testContact;
```

```
// Retrieve the contact from the database to ensure trigger logic
// is applied
Contact insertedContact = [SELECT Id, FirstName, LastName FROM
Contact WHERE Id = :testContact.Id];
// Verify that the trigger correctly set the standard field values
// using System.assert
    System.assert(insertedContact.FirstName == 'Max', 'FirstName
    should be set to "Max".');
    System.assert(insertedContact.LastName == 'Blank', 'LastName
    should be set to "Blank".');
    }
}
```

Step 2: Save new created test class and click the button "Run Test."

Step 3: Check the test result of the three methods in the tab "Test."

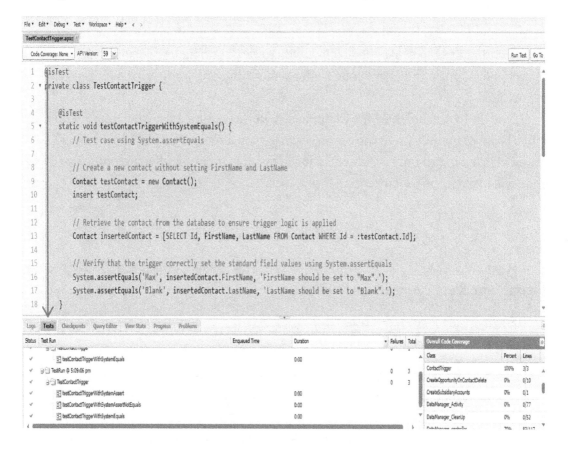

1. Use System.assertEquals method to ensure that the actual values match the expected values. If the values don't match, the test fails.

2. Use System.assertNotEquals method to ensure that the actual values do not match the unexpected values. If the values match, the test fails.

3. Use System.assert method with equality checks to verify that the actual values match the expected values. If the Boolean conditions are not met, the test fails. Note that System.assert is a more general assertion, and it can be used for various conditions beyond equality checks.

9.2 Try-Catch Method

In Apex, the Try-Catch method is used to handle exceptions that may occur during the execution of a block of code. It allows you to catch and handle specific types of exceptions, preventing your code from crashing and providing error handling capabilities.

If you try to execute the code example as follows without a try-catch block, and the index is out of bounds (as in the example where you attempt to access an element at index 10 in a list with only 5 elements), it will result in an unhandled exception, and your code will likely fail to execute.

```
// Define a list
List<Integer> numberList = new List<Integer>{1, 2, 3, 4, 5};

// Attempt to access an element at a specific index (index 10 in this case)
Integer element = numberList[10];

// Display the accessed element
System.debug('Element at index 10: ' + element);
```

If you run this code, it will throw an error at runtime, and your debug logs or console will show an error message indicating the issue. Using try-catch allows you to catch and handle such exceptions, preventing them from causing the entire program to fail and giving you the opportunity to take appropriate actions when an exceptional situation occurs.

To handle this issue you can adjust the catch block like this:

```
// Define a list
List<Integer> numberList = new List<Integer>{1, 2, 3, 4, 5};

try {
    // Access an element at a specific index (index 10 in this case)
    Integer element = numberList[10];

    // Display the accessed element
    System.debug('Element at index 10: ' + element);
} catch (Exception ex) {
    // Handle the exception
    System.debug('Exception caught: ' + ex.getMessage());
}
```

In this example, the numberList contains elements from index 0 to 5. However, we attempt to access an element at index 10, which is out of bounds. This will result in an error, and the try-catch block is used to catch and handle this exception.

This demonstrates how a try-catch block can be employed to gracefully handle situations where an index might be out of bounds in a list, preventing the program from failing due to an unhandled exception.

9.3 Test Data Factory

There are several ways to create test data in Apex test classes, including creating test data directly in the test class, using a factory class, or uploading test data into a static resource. The choice of method depends on the complexity of your test data requirements and your preferences for test data generation.

You can create test records directly within your test method as we've already done in our first test example for our TestContactTrigger class. This approach is suitable for simple test cases where you only need a few records to test a specific piece of functionality.

A factory class is a separate Apex class dedicated to creating test data. It's especially useful when you have complex data structures or need to create a large number of related records. It used to centralize and standardize the creation of test data, making it easier to maintain and reuse test data creation logic across multiple test classes with reusable methods for creating test records. It involves creating a public test class that is excluded from the organization code size limit and executes in a test context. To create a test data factory in Salesforce, you can follow the Test Data Factory pattern including creation of a public test class with the @isTest annotation and define static methods within the test class to create various types of test data.

Let's create our test data factory for the given ContactTrigger test class; follow these steps:

Step 1: Create the new class *ContactFactory* in your Developer Console.

```
@isTest
public class ContactFactory {
    public static Contact createContact(String firstName, String
    lastName) {
        Contact newContact = new Contact();
        newContact.FirstName = firstName;
```

```
        newContact.LastName = lastName;
        return newContact;
    }
}
```

Step 2: Modify our already created test class for the ContactTrigger, to use the methods from the *ContactFactory* class for test data creation.

```
@isTest
private class TestContactTrigger {

    @isTest
    static void testContactTriggerWithSystemEquals() {
        // Test case using System.assertEquals

        // Use the factory to create a contact
        Contact testContact = ContactFactory.createContact('Max', 'Blank');
        insert testContact;

        // Retrieve the contact from the database to ensure trigger logic
        // is applied
        Contact insertedContact = [SELECT Id, FirstName, LastName FROM
        Contact WHERE Id = :testContact.Id];

        // Verify that the trigger correctly set the standard field values
        // using System.assertEquals
            System.assertEquals('Max', insertedContact.FirstName,
            'FirstName should be set to "Max".');
            System.assertEquals('Blank', insertedContact.LastName,
            'LastName should be set to "Blank".');
    }

    @isTest
    static void testContactTriggerWithSystemAssertNotEquals() {
        // Test case using System.assertNotEquals

        // Use the factory to create a contact
        Contact testContact = ContactFactory.createContact('Max', 'Blank');
        insert testContact;
```

```
    // Retrieve the contact from the database to ensure trigger logic
    // is applied
    Contact insertedContact = [SELECT Id, FirstName, LastName FROM
    Contact WHERE Id = :testContact.Id];

    // Verify that the trigger did not set unexpected values
    // using System.assertNotEquals
    System.assertNotEquals('Unexpected Value', insertedContact.FirstName,
    'FirstName should not be "Unexpected Value".');
    System.assertNotEquals('Unexpected Value', insertedContact.LastName,
    'LastName should not be "Unexpected Value".');
}

@isTest
static void testContactTriggerWithSystemAssert() {
    // Test case using System.assert

    // Use the factory to create a contact
    Contact testContact = ContactFactory.createContact('Max', 'Blank');
    insert testContact;

    // Retrieve the contact from the database to ensure trigger logic
    // is applied
    Contact insertedContact = [SELECT Id, FirstName, LastName FROM
    Contact WHERE Id = :testContact.Id];
    // Verify that the trigger correctly set the standard field values
    // using System.assert
        System.assert(insertedContact.FirstName == 'Max',
        'FirstName should be set to "Max".');
        System.assert(insertedContact.LastName == 'Blank',
        'LastName should be set to "Blank".');
    }
}
```

In the provided example, the purpose of the ContactFactory is to encapsulate the logic of creating a new Contact instance with specified firstName and lastName values. The factory class simplifies the process of creating test data, making the test code more modular and readable.

You can run the test again in Developer Console as already described in our first test example and check the test results.

9.4 @TestSetup Method

The @TestSetup annotation in Apex is used to designate a method as a test setup method. A test setup method is responsible for creating test data that is shared across multiple test methods within the same test class. It helps to reduce duplication and improve the efficiency of test code.

When a test class has a test setup method, it runs once before any test methods in the class. The test setup method is used to create the required data for the test methods to run successfully. It is especially useful when you have multiple test methods that require the same set of data.

Here's an example that demonstrates the usage of @TestSetup:

```apex
@isTest
private class ContactTriggerTest {

    @TestSetup
    static void setupTestData() {
        // Create a test account
        Account testAccount = new Account(Name = 'Test Account');
        insert testAccount;

        // Create a test contact without setting standard field values

        Contact testContactWithoutValues = new Contact(
            FirstName = 'John',
            LastName = 'Doe',
            AccountId = testAccount.Id
        );
        insert testContactWithoutValues;
    }

    @isTest
    static void testContactTrigger() {
        // Get test data
        List<Contact> testContacts = [SELECT Id, FirstName, LastName FROM
        Contact];
```

```
    // Set up test data with desired field values
    List<Contact> updatedContacts = new List<Contact>();
    for (Contact con : testContacts) {
        con.FirstName = 'Max';
        con.LastName = 'Blank';
        updatedContacts.add(con);
    }

    // Update the contacts
    update updatedContacts;

    // Verify that standard field values are set by the trigger

    List<Contact> reloadedContacts = [SELECT Id, FirstName, LastName
    FROM Contact WHERE Id IN :testContacts];
    for (Contact con : reloadedContacts) {
        System.assertEquals('Max', con.FirstName);
        System.assertEquals('Blank', con.LastName);
    }
}

@isTest
static void testAnotherFunctionality() {
    // Since @TestSetup has already created test data, you can
    // use it here
    List<Contact> testContacts = [SELECT Id, FirstName, LastName FROM
    Contact];

    // Add your test logic here for another functionality
    // For example, you can update the test contacts with new values
    for (Contact con : testContacts) {
        con.Description = 'New Description';
    }

    // Update the contacts
    update testContacts;

    // Verify the results if needed
    // For example, you can query the updated contacts and assert
    // their new values
```

```
        List<Contact> updatedContacts = [SELECT Id, Description FROM
        Contact WHERE Id IN :testContacts];
        for (Contact con : updatedContacts) {
            System.assertEquals('New Description', con.Description);
        }
    }
}
```

In the @TestSetup method, you're creating a test account and a test contact without setting standard field values. So, it runs once before any test method in the class. The test account and contact created here serve as the common test data for the subsequent test methods in the same class.

Then two test methods *testContactTrigger* and *testAnotherFunctionality* use the test data created in @TestSetup for their respective test scenarios.

1. In testContactTrigger, you're updating the FirstName and LastName fields of the test contacts and verifying that a trigger on the Contact object correctly sets the standard field values. This method demonstrates testing a specific trigger functionality.

2. In testAnotherFunctionality, you're using the same set of test contacts to test another functionality updating the Description field. This method showcases how you can reuse the common test data created in setupTestData for testing additional functionalities without having to recreate the data.

Now, let's address the SeeAllData=true attribute. In Apex, the SeeAllData=true attribute is used to indicate that test methods should have access to all data in the organization, including the organization's existing data as in the following example.

```
@isTest(SeeAllData=true)
private class TestWithSeeAllData {

    // Using SeeAllData=true, so no @TestSetup method is required

    @isTest
    static void testContactTrigger() {
        // Get test data
        List<Contact> testContacts = [SELECT Id, FirstName, LastName FROM
        Contact];
```

```
    // Set up test data with desired field values
    List<Contact> updatedContacts = new List<Contact>();
    for (Contact con : testContacts) {
        con.FirstName = 'Max';
        con.LastName = 'Blank';
        updatedContacts.add(con);
    }

    // Update the contacts
    update updatedContacts;

    // Verify that standard field values are set by the trigger

    List<Contact> reloadedContacts = [SELECT Id, FirstName, LastName
    FROM Contact WHERE Id IN :testContacts];
    for (Contact con : reloadedContacts) {
        System.assertEquals('Max', con.FirstName);
        System.assertEquals('Blank', con.LastName);
    }
}

@isTest
static void testAnotherFunctionality() {
    // Get test data
    List<Contact> testContacts = [SELECT Id, FirstName, LastName FROM
    Contact];

    // Add your test logic here for another functionality
    // For example, you can update the test contacts with new values
    for (Contact con : testContacts) {
        con.Description = 'New Description';
    }

    // Update the contacts
    update testContacts;

    // Verify the results if needed
    // For example, you can query the updated contacts and assert
    // their new values
```

```
    List<Contact> updatedContacts = [SELECT Id, Description FROM
    Contact WHERE Id IN :testContacts];
    for (Contact con : updatedContacts) {
        System.assertEquals('New Description', con.Description);
    }
  }
}
```

In this modified example, I've removed the @TestSetup method because with
SeeAllData=true, the test methods can access all data in the org directly.

However, it is generally not recommended to use SeeAllData=true because it can lead
to test code dependency on specific data that may change over time. The @TestSetup
annotation and SeeAllData=true cannot be used together. When @TestSetup is used, it
automatically creates the required test data, so there is no need to access existing data
using SeeAllData=true. It is best practice to use @TestSetup to create the necessary
data for your tests, ensuring that your tests are self-contained and independent of
external data.

9.5 Test.startTest() and Test.stopTest() Methods

The Test.startTest() and Test.stopTest() methods in Salesforce Apex are used to delineate
a specific section of code within a test method. This is useful for isolating and measuring
the performance of a specific piece of code and for ensuring that asynchronous code,
such as Batch Apex or future methods, is executed within the test context in the following
example.

Step 1: You can create the new class *MyBatchClass* in Developer Console.

```
public class MyBatchClass implements Database.Batchable<sObject> {

    public Database.QueryLocator start(Database.BatchableContext context) {
        // Your query to retrieve the records to be processed
        String query =
        'SELECT Id, Email FROM Contact WHERE Email = null OR Email = \'\'';
        return Database.getQueryLocator(query);
    }
```

```
public void execute(Database.BatchableContext context,
List<Contact> contacts) {
    // Update contacts with a common Email value only if the Email
    // is empty
    for (Contact con : contacts) {
        if (String.isBlank(con.Email)) {
            con.Email = 'test@example.com';
            // Perform additional logic if needed
            // ...
        }
    }
    update contacts;
}

public void finish(Database.BatchableContext context) {
    // Optional: Add any finishing logic here
}
}
```

Step 2: Now you can create the test class *MyBatchClassTest* and run the test for it.

```
@isTest
private class MyBatchClassTest {

    @isTest
    static void testBatchClass() {
        // Create test data
        List<Contact> testContacts = new List<Contact>();
        for (Integer i = 0; i < 200; i++) {
            testContacts.add(new Contact(
                FirstName = 'Test',
                LastName = 'Contact' + i,
                Email = ''
            ));
        }
        insert testContacts;
```

```
// Start the test context
Test.startTest();

// Execute the batch job
MyBatchClass myBatch = new MyBatchClass();
Database.executeBatch(myBatch);

// Stop the test context
Test.stopTest();

// Verify the results
List<Contact> updatedContacts = [SELECT Id, Email FROM Contact
WHERE Email = 'test@example.com'];
System.assertEquals(testContacts.size(), updatedContacts.size(),
'Match the number of test contacts');

for (Contact con : updatedContacts) {
    System.assertEquals('test@example.com', con.Email,
    'Email should be updated to test@example.com');
}
    }
}
```

The provided Apex code is an example of Batch Apex, a mechanism for processing large datasets asynchronously. The MyBatchClass class updates contact records with empty email addresses to "test@example.com". The corresponding test class, MyBatchClassTest, creates test contacts, runs the batch job, and verifies the expected updates. The use of Test.startTest() and Test.stopTest() ensures proper testing of asynchronous behavior. This code structure allows for efficient processing of data in chunks, addressing governor limits and bulk data scenarios.

CHAPTER 10

Salesforce Developer Experience (DX)

10.1 Salesforce Environments

Salesforce provides different environments to support the various stages of software development, testing, and production for organizations. These environments are designed to help ensure that changes and updates to Salesforce configurations and customizations are thoroughly tested and validated before being deployed to the live, operational environment. Here's an overview of these different environments.

Full Copy Sandbox

A Full Copy Sandbox is typically used for comprehensive testing, quality assurance, and training purposes. It replicates your entire production org, including all data and metadata. It allows you to test changes and configurations in an environment that closely resembles your production org. This environment is useful for testing complex scenarios, large-scale data migrations, and performance testing.

Partial Copy Sandbox

A Partial Copy Sandbox is similar to a Full Copy Sandbox, but it contains a subset of your production data. It is useful for testing scenarios that require a representative sample of data, but not the entire dataset. This environment strikes a balance between having realistic data for testing and reducing the storage requirements. It is commonly used for functional testing, user acceptance testing, and load testing and typically come with a storage limit of 5 GB.

Developer Pro Sandbox

A Developer Pro Sandbox is a dedicated environment for individual developers or small teams. It provides a separate space for development and testing, allowing developers to work independently without affecting other developers' work. It is typically

© Konstantin Kapitanov 2024

K. Kapitanov, *Salesforce Developer I Certification*, Certification Study Companion Series, https://doi.org/10.1007/979-8-8688-0300-0_10

used for individual development and testing tasks, such as building new features, debugging code, and experimenting with configurations.

Production

The production environment is the live instance of your Salesforce org that is used by your end users. This is where your business processes run, and it contains your actual customer data. Deployments to the production environment should be carefully planned and tested in sandboxes before being promoted to production. It is important to ensure that the changes made in sandboxes do not negatively impact the functionality and stability of your production org.

Once your code has been thoroughly tested in the pre-deployment sandbox, you can use change sets to move metadata from the sandbox environment to the production org.

Change Sets is a Salesforce feature that allows you to deploy metadata changes from one Salesforce org to another. But a deployment connection is required between two Salesforce orgs to send change sets from one org to another. Change sets in Salesforce are primarily used to move customizations and configurations between related sandboxes and production orgs. Change sets cannot be sent between orgs that are not affiliated with a production org.

For example, you can use change sets to move changes from a sandbox to a production org, or between two sandboxes that are created from the same production org.

Dev Hub

Dev Hub is a feature in Salesforce that allows you to create and manage scratch orgs. It provides a centralized hub for managing your development environments and allows you to create and delete scratch orgs as needed. Scratch orgs are temporary, disposable orgs that can be used for development and testing purposes. They are typically used for short-term development projects, feature development, and automated testing.

A Scratch Org is a disposable, configurable, and source-driven Salesforce org that can be created and used for a specific development or testing task. It is typically used for short-term development projects, feature development, and automated testing.

To create a new Scratch Org go to Setup ➤ Type "Dev Hub" in the search field on the left menu.

10.2 Visual Studio Code and Salesforce CLI

Visual Studio Code (VS Code) is a lightweight and highly customizable source code editor developed by Microsoft. It is widely used by developers for various programming languages, and it supports a variety of extensions that enhance its functionality.

The Salesforce CLI is a command-line interface that allows developers to manage their Salesforce orgs and metadata from the terminal. It provides a set of commands for creating and managing Salesforce projects, deploying and retrieving metadata, running tests, and more.

The Salesforce Extensions for Visual Studio Code is a plugin that provides a set of tools for developing Salesforce applications in Visual Studio Code. It includes features such as code completion, syntax highlighting, debugging, and more. The plugin also integrates with the Salesforce CLI to provide a seamless development experience.

By using Visual Studio Code with Salesforce CLI, developers can have a streamlined development experience, benefit from features like code completion and syntax highlighting, and leverage the power of the Salesforce CLI for managing and deploying Salesforce applications.

10.3 How to Install

Here's a step-by-step guide to installing Visual Studio Code, Salesforce CLI, and the Visual Studio Code plugin for Salesforce development.

1. **Install Visual Studio Code**

   Visit the official Visual Studio Code website at `https://code.visualstudio.com/`.

Download the installer for your operating system (Windows, macOS, or Linux).

Run the installer and follow the on-screen instructions to complete the installation.

2. **Install Salesforce CLI**

Open a terminal or command prompt.

Visit the Salesforce CLI website at https://developer. salesforce.com/tools/sfdxcli.

Follow the instructions to download and install Salesforce CLI for your operating system.

3. **Configure Salesforce CLI**

Open a terminal or command prompt.

Run the command "sfdx force:auth:web:login" to authenticate with your Salesforce org.

Follow the instructions in the browser to log in and authorize the CLI.

4. **Install Visual Studio Code Plugin**

Step 1: Open Visual Studio Code.

Click on the Extensions icon on the left sidebar (or press Ctrl+Shift+X).

Search for "Salesforce Extension Pack" in the Extensions marketplace.

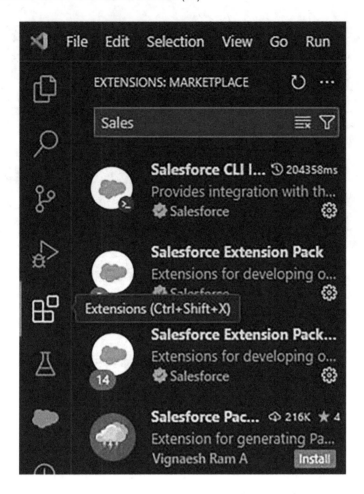

Step 2: Click "Install" on the Salesforce CLI and Salesforce Extension Pack.

Wait for the installation to complete.

Step 3: Connect Visual Studio Code to Salesforce Org:

Open a terminal or command prompt.

Run the command "sfdx force:auth:web:login --alias myAlias" to authenticate with your Salesforce org and set an alias for the org.

A browser window will open, prompting you to log in to your Salesforce org.

Log in with your Salesforce credentials.

The Salesforce CLI will exchange the code for an access token and a refresh token. Once the process is complete, the Salesforce alias will be stored in your local environment and can be used to connect to your org in Visual Studio Code.

CHAPTER 11

Salesforce Lightning Platform

11.1 Lightning Component Framework

Lightning Component framework is a previous development framework provided by Salesforce for building dynamic and responsive web applications and user interfaces on the Salesforce platform. The Aura framework is the underlying technology that powers the Lightning Component framework. It's a client-side framework that allows you to create reusable components, and it's a fundamental part of Salesforce's Lightning Experience, which provides a modern and streamlined user interface. The Lightning Component framework provides a lot of out-of-the-box components that can be reused, and it is an event-driven architecture. Components basic structure can contain HTML, CSS, JavaScript, SVG files, and Documentation.

Key features of the Lightning Component framework include

- *Component-Based Development*: The framework is based on a component-based development model, where developers can create reusable components that encapsulate functionality and can be easily combined to build complex applications.

- *Event-Driven Architecture*: Components in the Lightning Component framework communicate with each other using events, allowing for loose coupling and easier integration between components.

- *Easy Integration with Salesforce*: The Lightning Component framework integrates seamlessly with the Salesforce platform, allowing developers to leverage the full power of Salesforce's features and capabilities.

© Konstantin Kapitanov 2024
K. Kapitanov, *Salesforce Developer I Certification*, Certification Study Companion Series,
https://doi.org/10.1007/979-8-8688-0300-0_11

- *Responsive Design*: The framework provides responsive design capabilities, enabling applications to adapt and provide an optimal user experience across different screen sizes and devices.

- *Low-Code and Pro-code Tools*: Developers can use both low-code tools, such as Lightning App Builder, and pro-code tools, such as Apex, to increase productivity and customize applications according to specific business requirements.

- *Supported by Salesforce*: The Lightning Component framework is still actively supported by Salesforce, ensuring regular updates, bug fixes, and compatibility with the latest Salesforce releases.

However Lightning Web Components offer as a new standard several advantages over Lightning Components, including improved performance and better integration with modern web standards.

Visualforce is an older framework that was introduced by Salesforce before Lightning Components has been in use for many years. It's still used primarily with Salesforce Classic. It is based on the Model-View-Controller (MVC) architecture and uses a server-side rendering approach. But this topic is beyond the scope of this book.

11.2 Introducing the Lightning Web Components (LWC)

Lightning Web Components (LWC) is a UI framework developed by Salesforce for building web applications on the Salesforce platform. It was introduced as a new programming model for building Lightning components.

Prior to LWC, Salesforce developers primarily used Aura components, which were based on the Aura framework. While Aura components provided a powerful and flexible development environment, they also had some limitations in terms of performance and code reusability.

With the introduction of LWC, Salesforce aimed to provide a modern, lightweight, and efficient framework for building web components. LWC leverages standard web technologies like HTML, CSS, and JavaScript, and is built on top of the Web Components standard, which is supported by all major browsers.

LWC brings several advantages over Aura components, including improved performance, better code encapsulation, enhanced reusability, and improved debugging and testing capabilities. It also provides a more intuitive and developer-friendly programming model, making it easier to build and maintain complex applications.

Since its introduction, LWC has gained significant popularity and has become the recommended framework for building Lightning components.

LWC typically consists of three basic elements.

1. **HTML File**

   The HTML file defines the structure of the component's user interface. It includes the markup that determines how the component should be displayed to users. The HTML file has a ".html" extension.

2. **JavaScript (JS) File**

   The JavaScript file contains the logic and behavior of the component. It includes methods that handle events, process data, and interact with the component's lifecycle. The JavaScript file has a ".js" extension.

3. **js-meta.xml File**

   The js-meta.xml file is a metadata file that provides information about the Lightning web component. It includes details such as the component's name, description, and configuration settings. This file is crucial for defining metadata properties of the component. The js-meta.xml file has a ".xml" extension.

Here's a view of the directory structure in Visual Studio Code:

```
└── force-app\main\default
    └── lwc
        └── compoment
            └── __tests__
                ├── component.test.js
                ├── component.html
                ├── component.js
                ├── component.js-meta.xml
```

11.3 How to Create LWC

For the following example, you will need to install Visual Studio Code along with other Salesforce DX elements as described in the previous chapter.

Let us build a Lightning Web Component (LWC) that displays lead details and related changes based on the selected lead name from a picklist. It provides a user interface for selecting a lead name, fetching and displaying lead status details, and showing related changes associated with the selected lead.

So, you are here going through the steps:

Step 1: Open your Visual Studio Code application.

Step 2: On the top menu, go to View ➤ Command Palette.

- Type SFDX: and select Create Project.

- Select standard project template.

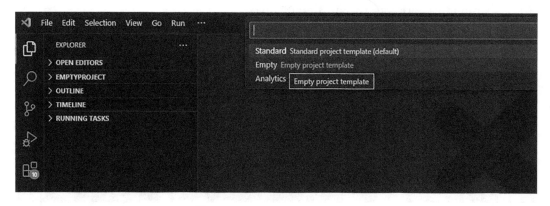

- Put the project name *"Project"* and press Enter. After your new project is created, you see the new elements on the left side.

Step 3: On the top menu, go to View ➤ Command Palette. Type SFDX: and select Create Lightning Web Component.

- Put the name *"leadChanges"*. Press enter. Choose standard suggested directory force-app\main\default\lwc.

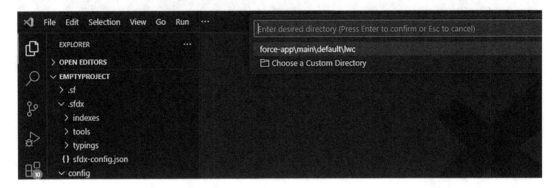

- After your lwc is created, you see the new directory on the left side consisting of leadChanges.html, leadChanges.js, and leadChanges. js-meta.xml files.

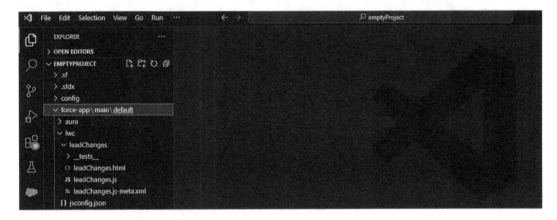

Now we need to change the sourcecode in the new created files.

Step 4: Select the file leadChanges.html file from your new created directory as on the preceding screenshot. Change the sourcecode of the file as follows and save the changes.

```
<template>
    <lightning-card title="Lead Changes" icon-name="standard:lead">
        <div class="slds-var-m-around_medium">
            <lightning-combobox
                label="Select Lead"
```

```
            value={leadRecord.Name}
            options={leadOptions}
            onchange={handleLeadChange}
        ></lightning-combobox>

        <p>Status: {leadRecord.Status}</p>

        <div class="slds-m-top_medium">
            <p>Related Changes:</p>
            <ul>
                <template for:each={relatedChanges} for:item="change">
                    <li key={change.Id}>{change.CreatedById.Name} -
                    {change.CreatedDate}</li>
                </template>
            </ul>
        </div>
    </div>
  </lightning-card>
</template>
```

The HTML file defines the structure and layout of the Lightning Web Component, including input fields, displayed information, and related changes. It complements the functionality implemented in the JavaScript file leadChanges.js and ensures a cohesive and well-designed user interface.

Step 5: Select the file leadChanges.js file from your new created directory as on the preceding screenshot. Change the sourcecode of the file as follows and save the changes.

```
import { LightningElement, track, api, wire } from 'lwc';
import getLeadDetails from
'@salesforce/apex/LeadController.getLeadDetails';
import getRelatedChanges from
'@salesforce/apex/LeadController.getRelatedChanges';
import getLeadPicklistValues from
'@salesforce/apex/LeadController.getLeadPicklistValues';

export default class LeadChanges extends LightningElement {
    @api leadId;
    @track leadRecord = { Name: '', Status: '', Id: '' };
```

```
@track relatedChanges = [];
@track leadOptions = [];

connectedCallback() {
    this.fetchLeadPicklistValues();
}

async fetchLeadPicklistValues() {
    try {
        const result = await getLeadPicklistValues();
        if (result) {
            this.leadOptions = result.map(option => ({ label: option,
            value: option }));
        }
    } catch (error) {
        console.error('Error fetching lead picklist values:', error);
    }
}

handleLeadChange(event) {
    this.leadRecord.Name = event.detail.value;
    this.fetchLeadDetails();
}

async fetchLeadDetails() {
    try {
        const result = await getLeadDetails({
        leadName: this.leadRecord.Name });
        if (result) {
            // Ensure we are setting the Status field
            this.leadRecord = { ...this.leadRecord, ...result };
            this.fetchRelatedChanges();
        } else {
            this.leadRecord.Status = 'Lead not found';
            this.relatedChanges = [];
        }
    } catch (error) {
```

```
            console.error('Error fetching Lead details:', error);
        }
    }

    async fetchRelatedChanges() {
        try {
            const result = await getRelatedChanges({
            leadId: this.leadRecord.Id });
            if (result) {
                this.relatedChanges = result;
            } else {
                this.relatedChanges = [];
            }
        } catch (error) {
            console.error('Error fetching related changes:', error);
        }
    }
}
```

Here are some key aspects of this example that reflect the modern LWC standard:

- The JavaScript file (leadChanges.js) uses the ES6 module syntax, allowing for better organization and encapsulation of code.

- Decorators such as @api and @track are used for defining public properties and tracking changes in the component's state.

- Asynchronous JavaScript features, such as async/await, are used to handle asynchronous operations, such as making server-side Apex method calls.

Step 6: Select the file leadChanges.js-meta-xml file from your new created directory as on the preceding screenshot. Change the sourcecode of the file as follows and save the changes.

```
<?xml version="1.0" encoding="UTF-8" ?>
<LightningComponentBundle xmlns:="http://soap.sforce.com/2006/04/metadata">
    <apiVersion>59.0</apiVersion>
    <isExposed>true</isExposed>
```

187

```
<targets>
    <target>lightning__AppPage</target>
    <target>lightning__RecordPage</target>
    <target>lightning__HomePage</target>
</targets>
</LightningComponentBundle>
```

LeadChanges.js-meta.xml configures the Lightning Web Component for Salesforce, specifying its API version, exposure in different Lightning contexts (App Page, Record Page, Home Page), and marking it as an exposed component.

Lightning Web Components (LWC) can interact with the server-side Apex controllers to perform various operations, such as querying data, updating records, and executing business logic. This interaction is typically done through Apex methods annotated with the @AuraEnabled annotation.

Step 7: Let's take the last step to create this controller class for our LWC. Open Developer Console in your Salesforce org. On the top menu, go to File ➤ New ➤ Apex Class. Put the name *"LeadController"*. Change the source code of the class file as follows and save the changes.

```
public with sharing class LeadController {
    @AuraEnabled(cacheable=true)
    public static List<String> getLeadPicklistValues() {
        List<String> leadPicklistValues = new List<String>();

        // Query distinct lead names
        for (Lead lead : [SELECT Name FROM Lead WHERE Name != null
        LIMIT 100]) {
            leadPicklistValues.add(lead.Name);
        }

        return leadPicklistValues;
    }

    @AuraEnabled(cacheable=true)
    public static Lead getLeadDetails(String leadName) {
        return [SELECT Id, Name, Status FROM Lead WHERE Name = :leadName
        LIMIT 1];
    }
```

```
@AuraEnabled(cacheable=true)
public static List<ChangeRecordWrapper> getRelatedChanges(Id leadId) {
    List<ChangeRecordWrapper> changeRecords =
    new List<ChangeRecordWrapper>();

    // Query the LeadChangeEvent records
    for (LeadChangeEvent event : (List<LeadChangeEvent>)
    Database.query('SELECT Id, CreatedById, CreatedDate'+
    'FROM LeadChangeEvent WHERE LeadId = :leadId ORDER BY'+
    'CreatedDate DESC LIMIT 5')) {
        ChangeRecordWrapper wrapper = new ChangeRecordWrapper(event);
        changeRecords.add(wrapper);
    }

    return changeRecords;
}

public class ChangeRecordWrapper {
    @AuraEnabled public Id Id { get; private set; }
    @AuraEnabled public String CreatedById { get; private set; }
    @AuraEnabled public Datetime CreatedDate { get; private set; }

    public ChangeRecordWrapper(LeadChangeEvent event) {
        this.Id = event.Id;
        this.CreatedById = event.CreatedById;
        this.CreatedDate = event.CreatedDate;
    }
}
}
```

The LeadController Apex class serves as a backend controller for our LWC. It utilizes common Apex practices, including executing SOQL queries with getLeadPicklistValues, getLeadDetails and employing for loops to populate lists of data. This enables the LWC to interact with the Salesforce server, retrieve lead information, and display it dynamically in the user interface.

11.4 Deployment in Salesforce Org

Now that we've created the Lightning Web Component (LWC) in Visual Studio Code and the new Apex class in the Developer Console, we're ready to proceed with deployment to use this LWC in your Salesforce org. First, ensure that you correctly connect the project with your selected Salesforce org.

Step 1: On the top menu, go to View ➤ Command Palette.

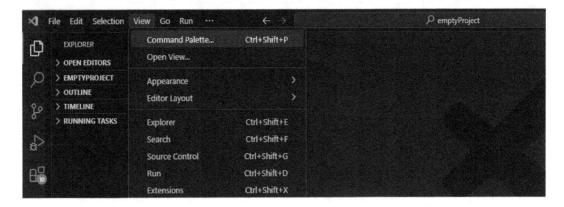

- Type SFDX: and select Authorize an Org.

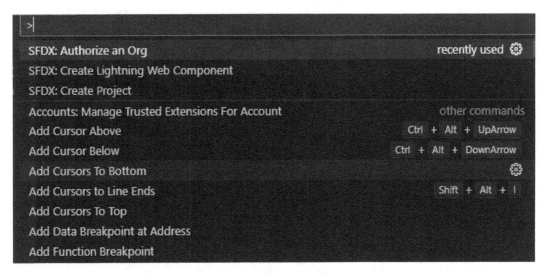

- Select Project Default

- Put your Salesforce org alias and press Enter. After your org is connected with new created project.

  Note! If you have already authorized an org and set it as the default using the CLI with an alias, you should configure your project to use this alias as the default org.

Step 2: Now select our created Lightning Web Component in the 'force-app\main\ default\lwc' directory ➤ right-click to open the context menu ➤ choose 'SFDX: Deploy Source to Org.

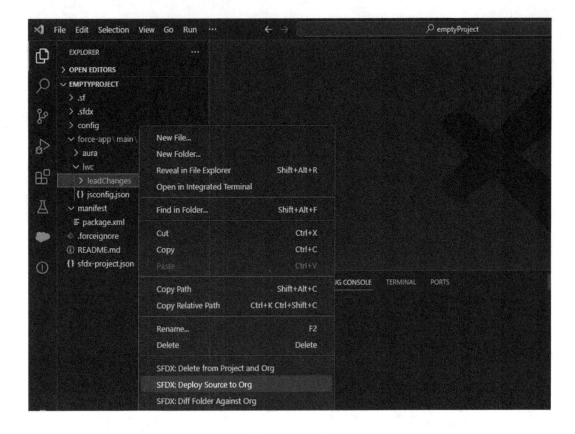

- After successful LWC deployment to your Salesforce org you will get an output like this.

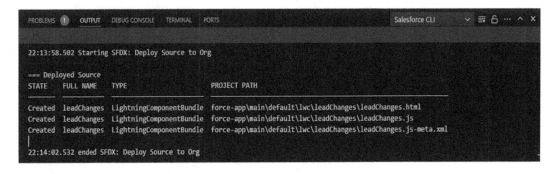

Step 3: Open your Salesforce Setup ➤ on the left menu, type "Lightning Components" in the search field ➤ open menu Lightning Components.

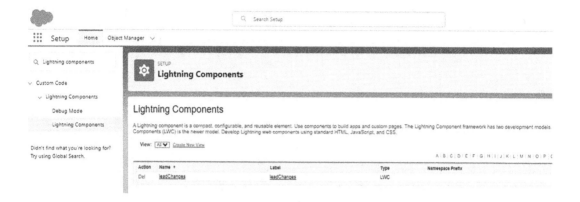

Now, you can view the list of your implemented components.

Step 4: Go to your Salesforce Home ➤ on the top right menu select Edit Page.

Step 5: Locate your deployed Lightning Web Component in the left menu under Custom ➤ simply drag and drop the component from the left menu onto the canvas ➤ click save botton on the right menu ➤ select the arrow at the top left of the menu to return to your homepage and view your implemented Lightning Web Component.

Now, you can select Leads from the list in the new created Lightning Web Component, and observe the lead status being automatically displayed.

By using the Mobile Tools from Salesforce via Microsoft Visual Studio Code, you can preview and debug your Lightning web components in the context of the Salesforce Mobile App. This allows you to ensure that your components function correctly and provide the expected user experience on mobile devices. For more informations go to `https://developer.salesforce.com/tools/mobile-debugging`.

11.5 Summary

This book covers many topics, but you can gain even more confidence by exploring additional examples and perspectives on the same subjects through Trailhead and completing the Developer I Trailmix `https://trailhead.salesforce.com/users/strailhead/trailmixes/prepare-for-your-salesforce-platform-developer-i-credential`.

As you conclude your journey with this book, you are now equipped with understanding of programming fundamentals and practical insights into the Salesforce platform. This knowledge not only prepares you for certification as a Salesforce Developer I but also empowers you to take the next steps in your career. By integrating these skills, you can confidently navigate the Salesforce ecosystem, leveraging its full capabilities to drive innovation and efficiency.

Embrace the opportunity to become more proficient in coding and deepen your involvement in the Salesforce community. Continue to explore, learn, and engage with the dynamic world of Salesforce, and let this book be the beginning of your ongoing journey toward mastery and success.

Index

© Konstantin Kapitanov 2024
K. Kapitanov, *Salesforce Developer I Certification*, Certification Study Companion Series,
https://doi.org/10.1007/979-8-8688-0300-0

INDEX

GPSR Compliance
The European Union's (EU) General Product Safety Regulation (GPSR) is a set
of rules that requires consumer products to be safe and our obligations to
ensure this.

If you have any concerns about our products, you can contact us on

ProductSafety@springernature.com

In case Publisher is established outside the EU, the EU authorized
representative is:

Springer Nature Customer Service Center GmbH
Europaplatz 3
69115 Heidelberg, Germany